D0095807

PRAYER FOR BEGINNERS

Brother Laurence
Practice of the Presence of God

PETER KREEFT

Prayer for Beginners

IGNATIUS PRESS   SAN FRANCISCO

Cover design by Roxanne Mei Lum

© 2000 Ignatius Press, San Francisco
ISBN 978-0-89870-775-5
Library of Congress catalogue number 99-75404
Printed in the United States of America ⊗

This book is dedicated
to the person who taught me to pray,
or rather *is* teaching me
(with astonishing patience),
Jesus Christ.

CONTENTS

INTRODUCTION

How This Book Is Different

There are thousands of books on how to pray, some of them very good ones. Why another? How is this one different?

Because this one could have been titled "Prayer for Dummies", prayer for people who are not very good at praying, people who find it hard to pray, not people who find it easy—in other words, people like me.

And it is also "prayer for Marthas", not for Marys: for people with little time to pray, busy people who keep finding excuses not to pray—in other words, people like me.

Much of it is based on principles found in Brother Lawrence's little classic *The Practice of the Presence of God*, which I have found the simplest, most practical book for beginners, for "dummies", and for "Marthas".

You would not be reading this book if you did not believe that prayer was worth working at, that real contact with God in prayer was something precious and powerful and worth your effort. But neither would you be reading this book if you *beginner's & practical*

had not experienced difficulty and failure in praying. What you need is not an advanced book on
prayer, or even an intermediate one, but a beginner's book. You also need a practical book, written by somebody like you, a beginner with the
same problems you have, somebody who knows
what *does not* work for busy, distracted, not-very-
holy people like you—and also knows something
that does.

NECESSITY

*Why Praying Is More
Important than Eating*

Eating keeps your body alive, and prayer keeps your soul alive. Praying is more important than eating because your soul is more important than your body. Your soul is more important than your body because your soul is you, your personality, your self. You will get a new body after death, in the resurrection at the end of the world. But you will not get a new soul; you will only purify and sanctify your old one, because you *are* your soul. The "you" that will get a new body *is* your soul.

Praying keeps your soul alive because prayer is real contact with God, and God is the life of the soul as the soul is the life of the body. If you do not pray, your soul will wither and die, just as, if you do not eat, your body will wither and die.

So a book that can make the difference between not praying and praying is a book that can change your life.

This book can change your life if and only if you do two things with it.

First, you must read it, not as you read other books, but *slowly* and *thoughtfully* (that is why I made it very short) and above all *prayerfully*, that is, under the eye of God, in the presence of Truth and therefore in absolute honesty.

Second, you must actually do it, not just read about doing it, think about doing it, understand how to do it, plan to do it, or imagine yourself doing it. It is a cookbook, not a dinner.

Do not be like the theologian who after death was given the choice between going to Heaven or going to a lecture on Heaven and chose the lecture.

Reading a book about doing something can be an obstacle to doing it because it gives you the impression that you are doing what you are only thinking about doing. It is tempting to remain in the comfortable theater of the imagination instead of the real world, to fall in love with the *idea* of becoming a saint and loving God and neighbor instead of doing the actual work, because the *idea* makes no demands on you. It is like a book on a shelf. But, as Dostoyevsky says, "love in action is a harsh and dreadful thing compared to love in dreams" (*The Brothers Karamazov*). A dream, or an idea, is a flattering addition to our mind; it does not demand any subtraction, any sacrifice of time and effort, as reality does.

One common cause of this mistake of preferring to imagine and admire a great ideal instead of beginning to do little deeds is our impatience with little baby steps, our lack of humility. In the real world we have to learn to crawl before we walk and walk before we run. This book does not teach you how to run, or even walk, at prayer; it teaches you how to crawl.

2

MOTIVES

Ten Compelling Reasons to Pray

1.) Why pray? Because *only prayer can save the world*

Some say that prayer, and "the spiritual life", or "the inner life", or the soul's private love affair with God, is an unaffordable luxury today, or an irresponsible withdrawal from the pressing public problems of our poor, hurting world. I say just the opposite: that nothing, *nothing* is more relevant and responsible; that nothing else can ever cure our sick world except saints, and saints are never made except by prayer.

Nothing but saints can save our world because the deepest root of all the world's diseases is sin, and saints are the antibodies that fight sin.

Nothing but prayer can make saints because nothing but God can make saints, and we meet God in prayer. Prayer is the hospital for souls where we meet Doctor God.

2. There is an even better reason to pray than the fact that only prayer can save the world. We must pray *because God commands it*

We pray, not simply as some solitary self-improvement program, but because we have been addressed by God. Prayer is a response to a prior divine invitation.

No, "invitation" is too weak. God *commands* us to pray, in fact to "pray constantly" (1 Thess 5:17). He yearns and longs for us to pray more passionately than any earthly lover yearns for his beloved to turn her eyes and her attention to him. (All earthly loves are tiny droplets of his infinite sea of love; he is where all love comes from, whether we receive it pure or whether we pollute it.)

We pray to obey God, not to "play God". We pray, not to change God's mind, but to change our own; not to command God, but to let God command us. We pray to "let God be God". Prayer is our obedience to God even when it asks God for things, for God has *commanded* us to ask (Mt 7:7).

3. But *why* did God command prayer? Whatever God does, he does for good reasons

Three reasons God commands us to pray correspond to our three deepest needs, the fundamental needs of the three powers of our soul: *prayer gives truth to our mind, goodness to our will, and beauty to our heart.* "The true, the good, and the beautiful" are the three things we need and love the most, because they are three attributes of God.

Prayer gives truth to our mind because it puts us in the presence of Truth itself, the divine Mind who designed our minds and our lives and our whole universe.

It gives goodness to our will because it puts us "on line" with God, in love with the God who *is* love and goodness. That is his essence. In prayer we become like the God we pray to and conform to; we catch the good infection of Godliness by contact.

It gives beauty to our heart because it plunges us into the heart of God, which is the eternal energy of infinite joy. That is why it gives us joy and peace and delight and happiness.

4. We should pray *because God's honor deserves it, in fact demands it*

To put it most simply, God is *God*, the Absolute Reality, Infinite Perfection, more massively real than the universe itself and more worthy than all the ideals together ever conceived by all human minds. If God is not this, then God is not God, but only something like Zeus, some finite thing in our world, or something like a good idea, some finite thing in our mind.

Thus, we should pray because prayer is the most realistic thing in the world to do. It is our acknowledgment of reality, our right response to reality, our honesty with reality. Right Response to Reality—the Three R's—is the fundamental principle of morality, of sanctity, and of sanity. We will see this with dazzling clarity in Heaven—that prayer is the right response to divine reality—and though we know it here only by faith, we do know it, and we had better practice it, because we need to rehearse now for what we will be doing forever in Heaven, if we want to be utterly practical and realistic.

5. Remembering the facts of death and Heaven gives us an even more pressing reason to learn to pray: *We do not have an infinite amount of time*

We are one day nearer Home today than we ever were before. I guarantee you that after you die you will *not* say "I spent too much time praying; I wish I had watched more TV instead."

We must learn to pray because infinite and uncompromising Love will not leave us alone until we do. If we do not learn to practice his presence with our whole mind and will in this life, we will have to learn it in Purgatory, where it will be much more painful—or else we will never learn

it, and that is Hell. That is why divine love made
Purgatory: to finish the job. (Divine love did not
make Hell; sin made Hell.) God's love by its un-
changeable nature must burn away all our imper-
fections as a great artist creates a masterpiece by
endless revisings and perfectings. It is his very nature to do so, as it is the nature of the sun to shine.
We are not wise to struggle against his nature!

Praying is like gardening: the growing of something alive—in this case, alive for eternity. It is
gradual, and it is invisible, but it is the difference
between life and death.

Prayer is plant food. This plant—your soul—is
going to be transplanted at death into an immor-
tal, eternal garden.

Learning to pray is dress rehearsal for eternal
life. What you do when you rehearse a play is
actually to practice it, to *do* it; and what we do
when we pray is actually to practice what we will
be doing in Heaven.

6. Prayer is *delightful*

Brother Lawrence says, in *The Practice of the Presence of God*, "There is not in the world a kind
of life more sweet and delightful than that of a
continual conversation with God. Those only can
comprehend it who practice and experience it"
(Letter 5). No one who has ever tried it has ever
given it a lesser rating than that. For even though

our prayer-contact with God may be almost infinitely poor, the God we thus contact is infinitely rich! Therefore "we are to be pitied who content ourselves with so little. God has infinite treasure to bestow" (Letter 4). What is that? "What no eye has seen, nor ear heard, nor the heart of man conceived, what God has prepared for those who love him" (1 Cor 2:9).

Delight is a subjective reason for praying, but it is a valid one. The ideal of being motivated by the objectively better reasons—practicing for Heaven, God's honor, obedience to his command, honesty, and realism—is the *goal* of prayer; but it does not have to be the *beginning*. God accepts the more "selfish" and subjective but natural motive of our own delight and peace and joy and happiness as perfectly proper, for God appeals to this motive throughout Scripture. He is not an elitist; he stoops to conquer. He stoops down even into the spiritual nursery and carefully watches over spiritual infants like us. We must not try to be more pure and high-minded than our Father! God is indeed a perfectionist about our end ("You . . . must be perfect, as your heavenly Father is perfect" [Mt 5:48]), but he is a pragmatist about our beginning. Like a good earthly father, he is "easy to please but hard to satisfy" (C. S. Lewis, quoting George Macdonald).

7. Prayer is *the way to know God*, and this is Jesus' definition of eternal life: "This is eternal life: that they know thee, the only true God" (Jn 17:3)

To know anyone, you must not just know thousands of things *about* him, but you must know *him*, you must *meet* him, you must spend time with him, or, as Brother Lawrence would say, "practice his presence". The same is true of knowing God. To pray is to know God by practicing his presence; and this is to live in reality (for God *is* really present), instead of in the fantasy worlds we construct in our own minds, in which God is absent.

One moment of prayer, of weak worship, confused contrition, tepid thanksgiving, or pitiful petition will bring us closer to God than all the books of theology in the world. Saint James says, sarcastically, "So you know that there is one God? Oh, good for you! The demons also know that, but tremble with fear" (James 2:19, my paraphrase). Job's three friends said nothing but theologically correct truths, while Job was so hurt, desperate, and confused that he wondered whether God was really just (Job 9:17–24). Yet God was angry at the three friends and said to them, "You have not spoken rightly before me, as my servant Job has" (Job 42:7, JB). For while the three friends spoke only truths *about* God, Job spoke *to* God. He prayed.

Effect of prayer is knowing God.

8. Prayer, and its effect, knowing God, is *the essential prerequisite for all religious teachers*, catechists, evangelists, and preachers

For the thing that all we fallen sons of Adam and daughters of Eve most deeply need (and also, deep down, *know* that we need, even if we deny this knowledge with our words) is not a knowledge about God but a knowledge of God. Where is the teacher who knows God, knows him by being in love with him? The most cynical and rebellious sinner will be silent before such a teacher.

9. Prayer is *the only way to spiritual progress*

Human lovers often say to each other, "If I did not love you more today than I did yesterday, I would love you less. And that is intolerable. So I must find more ways to love you every day." Brother Lawrence says, "Not to advance in the spiritual life is to go back" (Letter 4).

For we are not sitting still, merely thinking about moving closer to God; we are moving all the time, in our spirit as well as our body. Even thinking takes time; though it is not in space, like our body, it is in time, like our body. We may think we are sitting still, but that is at every moment an illusion, both physically and spiritually. Physically, this "stable" earth is really a spaceship moving at alarming speed down four paths at once: rotating around its own axis, revolving around its sun with

rotate
revolve around sun
spiraling around galaxy
spiraling out in

22   PRAYER FOR BEGINNERS   expanding
                                        universe

the rest of the solar system, spiraling around its
galaxy with other suns and solar systems, and spiraling out into the ever-expanding universe with
the rest of its galaxy. Spiritually, however, our mo-
tion is linear: with every choice we move either
closer to God or farther away from him. For while
our physical universe is round and relative, our
spiritual universe is not. It has an Absolute.

If we are "in Christ", we are moving with the
most pressing speed, for we are "in" the most dy-
namic man who ever walked the earth. When he
says to us, "Follow me" (Mt 8:22), he is not saying, "Please remember to be nice." He is inviting
us to a high-speed chase down the roads of our
life. On that chase there is no rest except eternal
rest and no security except eternal security.

He will not leave us alone. His last words to us
were: "Lo, I am with you always" (Mt 28:20). We
usually interpret that saying as something sooth-
ing, like a pillow, but its Speaker was the home-
less wanderer who said of himself, "Foxes have
holes, and birds of the air have nests; but the Son
of man has nowhere to lay his head" (Mt 8:20).

We must pray in order to grow, and we must
grow because Infinite Love will not, cannot, settle
for less than the greatest joy of which his beloved
creature is capable. Even good earthly fathers want
the very best for their children; why do we expect
our Heavenly Father to be any less demanding and

leave us alone? That is what uncles do, not fathers. Christ did not teach us to pray, "Our Uncle who art in Heaven."

10. Prayer is necessary because without it we cannot attain *the meaning of life, the end and purpose of our existence*

Becoming saints is the meaning of life. It is why we exist. It is why God created us. It is the reason he banged out the Big Bang, and why he waited eighteen million years for human life to evolve, and why he providentially provided this one perfect planet, and why he breathed his Spirit into the Adam he formed out of its dust, and why he does the same to every baby conceived, and why he prepared a chosen people, and sent prophets among them, and finally came down from Heaven into a mother and a manger and a Cross, and was forsaken by God so that we need never be forsaken, and rose again, and sent his Spirit to haunt our hearts—all this stupendous effort was for one end: to make saints, to make little Christs, to give his Son brothers and sisters. The whole universe is a saint-making machine. And prayer is the fuel that powers it.

He was not called "Jesus" (Savior) merely because he was to save us from the *punishment* for our sins; he was called "Jesus" "for he will save his people from their sins" (Mt 1:21). His purpose was not just to make us *safe* but to make us *saints*.

Prayer is our first step in becoming saints. The second step is charity, a life of love, the ecstasy of giving ourselves away over and over again forever, as each of the Persons of the Trinity do. But this is prayer too, or the extension of prayer. This is practicing the presence of God in action.

Beautiful

3

METHODS

Why We Need None

But *how* should we pray?

Prayer is easier than we think. We want to think it is too hard or too high and holy for us, because that gives us an excuse for not doing it. This is false humility. We can all do it, even the most sinful, shallow, silly, and stupid of us.

You do not have to master some mystical method. You do not have to master any method at all. Can you talk to a friend? Then you can talk to God, for he is your Friend. And that is what prayer is.

You do not have to wait until you become a saint. This is the *way* to become a saint.

The single most important piece of advice about prayer is one word: Begin!

God makes it easy to begin: just do it! God also makes it easy to progress in prayer, for he rewards our efforts with peace and joy. And he makes it easiest of all at the end, for it gradually becomes more natural and more delightful. In fact,

funny

in Heaven, prayer will be more delightful than sex is now.

Life contains many hardships and pains, but prayer is not one of them.

Prayer is so simple that no method at all is needed. For some people, methods of prayer are of some help. For other people, they are more of a hindrance than a help. For no people at all are they the essential, substantive answer to the question of How.

Why is that? Because a "method" means a "technique", and a technique means a means to attain an end, a way of changing causes so as to change effects, a way of doing one thing (the means) so that by this means a second thing (the end) is done. For instance, pushing a button to make the light go on. We use such means only when they are easier than the end. We push a button to make the light go on in our house; we do not carry burning lava halfway around the world and put it into our house just to make the light go on there. That is why we use means or methods or techniques: to bring about a harder thing (the end) by means of an easier thing (the means).

Prayer is love. To love anyone is to seek his presence, to seek intimacy and union. (You do not love someone if you do not want to spend time with him.) Love is also communication. (You do not love someone if you do not want to talk with him and get to know him better.)

But love is too simple, too free, and too great for technology. There can be no technique for love, no "method" for loving.

Love is too simple for methods because it comes from the heart, the center of the self, which is like the point at the center of a circle.

Love is too free for methods because my love is my choice, and my choice cannot be made by anyone else (though others can help me). My love can be a *response* to yours, but it cannot be *caused* by yours. I can cause a Coke machine to give me a Coke, but I cannot cause you to love me. Even God cannot make us love him. "Forced love" is a meaningless impossibility, like "virtuous sin".

Love is too great for methods because the effect cannot be greater than the cause, and since nothing is greater than love, nothing can cause love except love itself. You "just do it".

We will suggest three simple *structures* for prayer —one in one step, one in three steps, and one in four steps—in the following chapters, but these are not *methods*. The only advice Jesus ever gave us about prayer was not a method but a structure, a model prayer (the "Lord's Prayer").

4

WORDS

Vocal Prayer as Conversation with God

Not all prayer is in words, because not all conversation is in words. But it begins with words. It is true that it goes beyond words, because it is love. It is true, as John Bunyan said, that God infinitely prefers a heart without words to words without a heart when we pray. But the road to wordless prayer is paved with words. The practice of God's presence without words (which is called "contemplative prayer" or "mental prayer" as distinct from "vocal prayer") will come in its time, but it will come only through the practice of vocal prayer. The wordless sense of God's presence is a flower that grows from the plant of prayer in words. For before we can "pray constantly" (1 Thess 5:17), we must first begin to pray!

We should not despise the simple, humble beginnings of prayer in words. Jesus did not. When asked "Teach us to pray", he gave us a vocal prayer.

We should use our own words, too, of course.

Our conversation with God should be utterly free and familiar, because God is the only person who will never, ever misunderstand us and never, ever reject us (hate us, ignore us, or be indifferent to us). These are the two reasons we hide from other people, even our friends, even our parents, and the two reasons we should never hide from God. "For my father and my mother have forsaken me, but the LORD will take me up" (Ps 27:10). We can tell him *everything*. For he *is* our everything.

But this "free and familiar" conversation is not idle *chatter*. It is not flip and casual. God is not our pet or our pop psychologist. God is *God*: utterly awesome, infinitely great. The familiarity of prayer is wonderful because it is familiarity with *God*.

There is absolutely no contradiction between saying we come to God freely and *familiarly* and saying we do not come *casually*. When spouses make love, it is not casual, like making jokes; yet it is utterly free and familiar and intimate, not inhibited and strange and at-a-distance.

There is also no contradiction between the familiarity and spontaneity of this continual conversation with God and our use of formal prayers and public liturgy. When we use the prayers of the Church, we use the greatest prayers ever written, the words and sentiments of great saints and hymn writers and liturgists. We do this rightly, because God deserves the best, and these prayers are the best. They were composed by other people, but we make them our own when we pray them, like a lover reciting a sonnet by Shakespeare to his beloved. It is Shakespeare's gift: Shakespeare gave it to him, and now he gives it to his beloved.

But if others' words are the *only* words lovers use to each other, they are not lovers but performers. We must not only "say our prayers", we must *pray*. Others' words may be more beautiful, but your words are more yours, and God cherishes them as a father cherishes his child's own crude drawing made just for him more than he cherishes the greatest work of art in the world. God wants your own words most of all because they are your own; they come from your heart, and your heart is what your Lover craves. Your heart may be paltry compared with the heart of a great saint, but *your* heart is what God wants from *you*. Your heart is all you can give him; you cannot give him the heart of a great saint. Until you become one, that is. And you become one only by giving him your heart.

5

STEPS

Stop, Look, and Listen

method sort of

This is the closest we will come to teaching a "method" of prayer. But these three steps are such a simple "method" that you will never forget them.

"Stop, look, and listen" is what you do at a railroad crossing. Prayer is like a railroad crossing. God is like a great train crossing the tracks of your life. You *want* to get run over by this train! So here is how you put yourself on the tracks in front of God.

First, STOP! Stop doing everything else you are doing. Stop worrying about anything else in the whole world except your prayer to God right now. Stop being Martha; if you don't, you cannot be Mary (see Lk 10:38–41). You cannot sit at the Lord's feet while you are running around on your own feet. You cannot hear him if you are frothing at the mouth and fussing at the fingers. You cannot LOOK unless you first STOP; you cannot practice the presence of God if you are just too busy for him.

This is true even of your kids and your parents: they need your time more than they need anything else, for that is your life—your life-time. Time is a test of love, and the beloved (or the not-beloved) always knows it. God certainly knows it.

You cannot "do God" by halves. God—the real God as distinct from some convenient man-made idea—is too big to fit into some little side slot in your mind while you are doing something else that is more important to you. He is not background music.

This first step, STOP, is in itself the easiest one. But you will probably find it the hardest if you are a typically modern American: busy, active, outgoing. Most of us are like rolling stones: we have too much momentum to slow down. If you do find this hard, remember that it is only hard to you; in itself it is easy. And remember that it is necessary: you have to stop even to smell the roses; all the more necessary to stop to talk to God!

The second step is LOOK: look at God with the eye of your soul, the eye of your mind. I mean the eye of faith. You cannot see God with your body's eye, and the eye of your reason is very weak; but the eye of faith is strong because that is God's own gift to you, the eye God provided.

Faith knows that God is real, and faith knows that God is present.

LOOK means simply LOOK. It is hard only because it is so simple. The holy Curé of Ars once noticed an old peasant praying alone in church every day before the Eucharist. The Curé asked the peasant what he did when he prayed, and his answer was the most perfect description of contemplative prayer: "I look at him, and he looks at me" (*Catechism of the Catholic Church* [CCC] 2715).

That is all. By a simple act of will, turn your attention to him. You cannot talk to someone if you do not look at him.

And this is going to be a two-way conversation. You are going to talk, but you are also going to listen. And you cannot listen to him unless you first look at him.

So the last step is LISTEN.

In a conversation, if you are the wisest, it makes sense for you to do most of the talking. If the other person is wiser, it makes sense for you to do most of the listening. The wiser the other is, the more listening you want to do. Well, prayer is conversation with God, and it makes no sense for us to do most of the talking. We ought to be listening most of the time.

But, you may object, we cannot hear God's voice as we can hear the voice of another human

ways to listen

being. True, but we can hear God's voice in other ways. We hear him in nature, which is his art. We hear him in his providential directing of our lives, and in the lessons in human history, and in the "still, small voice" of our conscience, God's interior prophet. We hear him loud and clear in Scripture, his inspired Word deliberately given to us. One way of praying is listening to God's voice in Scripture, reading Scripture as God's Word—which is exactly what it is!

And the best listening, the listening that gets the closest to God's heart, the listening that hears the most total revelation of God, is listening to Christ, God incarnate, God in the flesh, "very God of very God". "The Word of God" means the Bible only secondarily; primarily it means Christ. In the words of the *Catechism*, Christ is "the Father's one, perfect, and unsurpassable Word. In him he has said everything; there will be no other word than this one" (CCC 65). Praying by reading the Gospels prayerfully and "listeningly" is one of the very best ways to pray.

We also need to hear what God says to us at each moment of our lives. This is a habit we gradually develop, for God's voice is "a still, small voice". But he promised that we would learn to recognize it: "The sheep hear his voice, and he calls his own sheep by name . . . and the sheep follow him, for they know his voice" (Jn 10:3–4).

How do we listen to his voice? With the ear of our heart. With love. Love has ears, as love has eyes. Just be there, and love him, and let him love you.

What will happen then? What will we hear? Let God take care of that. Seek only him, do not use him as a means to seek any other end. He is not your Santa, he is your Savior. I cannot tell you what he will give you, except for one thing: he will give you himself. He will give you more of himself the more you want him, that is, the more you love him. He wants to pour infinite riches into your soul; prayer is a way of opening up your soul so that more of God can enter.

In order to listen, we must look. In order to look, we must stop. And in order to stop doing things, we must first be doing things. God gave us a world in which we are to work. But God also gave us a Sabbath, in which we are to pray. Why is the first third of this prayer—stopping— the hardest? Is your other work really so important that you cannot stop it for one Sabbath part out of seven to turn to the One who *gave* you your other work, in fact who gave you your very existence? You can pray the "stop, look, and listen" prayer in just one minute; can you not give God just one minute? The first minute of each hour? One part of our sixty? Is that too much of a Sabbath rest for you?

It is a simple, easy, and beautiful practice, and I absolutely guarantee you that if you do it, you will love it and cherish it and be very grateful for the suggestion.

Can you stop reading this right now and pray for one minute? If you cannot, you are in serious trouble; you are addicted to work and action as to a drug. You are a slave. If you can but you will not, you are in even more serious trouble; for that means that you do not love God as much as you love whatever else you are doing. Perhaps what you are doing is reading about loving God! So you have no time to love God because you are reading about loving God? That is insane.

We are all insane. That is what original sin means. Sin is insanity. It is preferring finite joy to infinite joy, creatures to the Creator, an unhappy, Godless self to a happy, God-filled self. Only God can save us from this disease. That is what the name "Jesus" means: "God saves." He has done his part, on the Cross. Our part is to accept him.

A good way to act out our acceptance right now would be to stop reading this book and pray for at least one minute. Will you give God one minute? Please do not give me, the author of these words, that minute and rob God. Please rob me and give it to God. Stop reading me and read God. Stop listening to me and listen to God.

Are you finished? Do not read another word until you are.

Now ask God to help you do that again and again for the rest of your life.

6

THOUGHTS

Where the Action Is

We usually *contrast* thought and action and divide people into "thinkers" and "doers". This is an illusion. For:

> Sow a thought, reap an act;
> Sow an act, reap a habit;
> Sow a habit, reap a character;
> Sow a character, reap a destiny.

The practice of the presence of God in prayer is not the end of sanctity, but it is its beginning. It leads to acts, and habits, and character, and destiny. It is not sufficient, but it is necessary.

Buddha was no theologian, but he was a brilliant psychologist, and he understood the primary importance of thought. The first line of the most popular Buddhist scripture, the *Dhammapada*, says: "All that we are depends on our thoughts. It begins where our thoughts begin, it moves where our thoughts move, it ends where our thoughts end."

The reason for the primacy of thought is very simple and very profound. It is that we are not merely animal organisms, not merely material creatures, but we have spiritual souls. Material beings are moved from without, like billiard balls; but spiritual beings are moved from within. The first cause of a specifically human act is always internal, not external. By "a specifically human act" I mean one like asking a question, creating a work of art, making a moral choice, affirming another person, or appreciating the beauty of nature—or praying. Mind moves itself from within, actively; matter is moved from without, passively. That is why thought is where the action starts.

Saint Paul knew this principle too. He knew that in order to become saints, in order to bring our whole lives into captivity to Christ, we must first "take every thought captive to obey Christ" (2 Cor 10:5).

The point and purpose of life is to become a saint, to become Christlike. Léon Bloy wrote: "Life holds only one tragedy: not to have been a saint."

There are two parts to the process of sanctification, or saint-making—the mind and the will —because they are the two powers of the human soul by which it resembles God. The heart of sanctity is in the heart, or the will, not in the mind; a saint is essentially one who loves God with his whole heart. But the heart cannot work without the mind. Mind and heart each depend on the other, like the chicken and the egg, or the senses and the intellect, or male and female.

Let us see how the mind and the heart (will) are dependent on each other in prayer.

First, the will must command the mind. That act of the mind that makes us aware of God's presence—how does it come about? Only by our willing it. Jesus tells us, "Seek and you shall find." *Seeking* is an act of the *will*: we seek what we will, what we want, what we love. *Finding* God is an act of the *mind*—not just the logical mind, of course, and not just by abstract ideas, but knowing *God*, personal knowing (*kennen*, not *wissen*, in German; *connaître*, not *savoir*, in French).

In order to *get* the awareness of God's presence, we must first *want* it, and seek it, and be willing to sacrifice for it. The mind will "stop, look, and listen" only when it is commanded to do so by the will. We will not listen to God if we do not look at God, and we will not look at him if we do not stop looking elsewhere, and we will not stop looking elsewhere without a deliberate choice of the will.

But the other half of the picture is also true: when we do practice the presence of God with our mind, it has profound effects on our will. For the more we know him (with our mind), the more reasons we have to love him (with our will), and serve him, and submit to his beauty. The more we get to know him, the more willing we are to sacrifice and suffer anything for him. Once you really know him, you will do *anything* for him, simply because of who he is.

As love and knowledge cause each other, so do their opposites, indifference and ignorance. (Indifference is more truly the opposite of love than hate is, for we can both love and hate the same person at the same time, but we cannot both love and be indifferent to the same person at the same time.) Just as the love of God makes us know him better, and the knowledge of God makes us love him better, so indifference to God makes us ignorant of him, and ignorance of him makes us indifferent.

So the battle begins here. Thought is the first battlefield.

7

FAITH

The One Prerequisite for Prayer   Faith

How do we know we are not fooling ourselves in prayer? How do we know God is really present and aware of us and interested in us?

(1) We cannot see him with our eyes. (2) We do not usually *feel* him or experience him with our emotions. (3) And we cannot rationally *prove* that he cares about us, that he has freely chosen to be present to us. We may be able rationally to prove God's existence, but we cannot rationally prove that he loves us; for his existence is necessary, but his love is his free gift, his free choice.

We know he is present because he has promised it: "Lo, I am with you always" (Mt 28:20). In other words, we know it by *faith*.

What is faith? Faith is not some state of mind we work up in ourselves. Faith is simply believing God's promises. Faith is relative to its object, God. Faith is not *in* us so much as it is *between* us and God. It is our response to God's initiative.

Faith is very simple. Faith says, "God said it, and I believe it, and that settles it." This is not mindless fundamentalism; this is utterly reasonable. For God can neither deceive nor be deceived. In the words of the old hymn, "If our faith were but more simple, we would take him at his word." Jesus gave us a little child, not an adult, as his chosen example of faith (Mk 10:15) and went so far as to say that unless we become like little children, we cannot enter his kingdom (Mt 18:3; Mk 10:15).

If we rely on anything else besides faith to maintain the practice of the presence of God, we will certainly fail, whether this is our feelings, or experiences, or sincerity, or good intentions, or reasonings, or plans. The reason these things will fail while faith will not fail is that all these things depend on us, while faith depends on God. It is a gift of God. We are free to accept or refuse the gift, but it is a gift of God, it is not our own self-created thing.

There is a great chasm between ourselves and God, between our subjective unawareness of his presence and the objective truth that he *is* present, between our darkness and his light. We cannot go from our darkness to his light, because we are working in the dark. But God can go from his light to our darkness, because he is working in

the light. Any bridge *we* try to build across that
infinite chasm between ourselves and God will
break, because we cannot bridge an infinite abyss
by finite power. But the bridge *God* builds to *us*
is unbreakable, for it is made by his power. That
bridge is Christ. We receive Christ by faith. And
even our faith in Christ, like Christ himself, is
God's gift to us. He gives us not only himself but
also a new organ to receive him with, a new eye
to see him with: the eye of faith.

Many people today want "experiences". Their
prayer is really, "Lord, I believe; help my bad feelings" instead of "Lord, I believe; help my unbe-
lief" (see Mk 9:24).

Faith is a *knowing*; faith's object is divine fact.
Faith is not a feeling, and faith's object is not
feelings. According to an ancient Chinese parable, Fact, Faith, and Feeling were walking along a
wall. As long as Faith kept his eyes ahead of him
on Fact, all three made progress. But when Faith
took his eyes off Fact and turned around to see
how Feeling was doing, Faith fell off the wall, and
Feeling fell with him, while Fact went on.

God trains us to rely on faith, not feeling or
sight or proof, by giving us the sacraments, especially the Eucharist. The Eucharist does not feel
like Christ, and it does not look like Christ, and
it cannot be proved to be Christ. But it is Christ.

God could easily have manifested his presence

to our eyes with dazzling signs and wonders, a
continual Mount of Transfiguration (Mt 17). He
could also have manifested himself to our feelings,
with an inward assurance of his presence so strong
that each time we received the Eucharist we felt
on top of the mountain. Instead, he hides himself.
This is a much harder thing for him to do than to
reveal himself, because it is like the sun finding a
way to hide its light.

So true

Why does he hide? To tempt us out of hiding,
as we might win the confidence of a fearful, foolish animal. Thus our faith is tested, trained, exer-
cised, and strengthened, like a muscle. We learn
no longer to lean on the crutches of feeling. Feelings are wonderful decorations, but they are not
a foundation to build on. They are dessert, not
bread or meat.

In his hymn "Adore Te", Saint Thomas Aquinas
says to Christ in the Eucharist:

> Sight, taste, and touch in Thee are each
>   deceived;
> The ear alone most safely is believed.
> I believe all the Son of God has spoken;
> Than Truth's own word there is no truer
>   token.

So true

So the most sophisticated and brilliant mind in
the history of theology is saying he believes in the
Real Presence of Christ in the Eucharist because

"God said it, and I believe it, and that settles it."
That childlikeness is the most advanced lesson in
faith. And it is what we must rely on in order
to succeed in practicing the presence of God in
prayer, where he is also hidden, as he is in the
Eucharist.

This reliance on faith will become even more
crucial when we move from the mind to the
will (in the last half of this book). For the foe
there is far more formidable. When we are on
the front porch of sanctity, the mind, we face
only the little lizards of laziness, distractions, and
doubts. But when we enter the living room and
hearth of sanctity, we face fire dragons and sala-
manders: cowardice, the fear of suffering and sacrifice, the desire to be in control (which we mislabel
"freedom"), self-righteousness (which we mislabel "self-esteem"), pride, and despair. Only faith
can sustain us then, as only faith sustained Christ
on the Cross when for the first time he no longer
felt his Father's presence and cried out in hellish
horror: "My God, my God, why hast thou forsaken me?" (Mt 27:46).

Only naked faith sustained him then. What kept
him on the Cross was not the nails, for he could
have called on twelve legions of angels to take
him down. His people said, "Come down from
the Cross and we will believe in you." But if he
had come down from the Cross, he would have
made it *impossible* for them to believe in him, for

he would have substituted sight for faith. That is why he does not take us down from our crosses: so that we do not substitute feelings and experiences for faith. He wants the very best for us, the strongest and most precious gift, and that is faith. Therefore he hides his presence from us *so that we can practice* his presence by faith. This hiding is one of his most precious gifts, and one for which he is hardly ever thanked.

Faith is required for prayer because we do not see, feel, or prove God. Faith's two children, hope and love, are also required. Hope is required because the only reason we expect our prayer will "count" is because God has promised it. Love is required because we would not *want* to do what prayer does, get close to God and bring God closer to us, if we did not love him. We do not invoke the presence of what we hate!

But that is all prayer requires: faith, hope, and love. Great holiness, or piety, or sanctity are not required. Prayer is a road *to* holiness; if holiness were a prerequisite, we would have a Catch-22 situation, like the young job applicant who cannot get a first job because every employer wants someone with work experience. You cannot get a job unless you have experience, but you cannot get experience unless you get a job!

All Christians can meet the three requirements of prayer, even the least holy. All who want to pray can.

Prayer is a road to holiness.

8

THEMES

What Should I Say When I Pray?

What should I say when I pray? To answer this question, let's ask a more basic one: What do we do when we pray?

We practice the presence of God.

And who is God? What is God?

God is infinite love. That is why prayer is not boring. Are you bored when you are in the presence of the human being you love the most? Love is the only thing in this life that definitively and triumphantly answers the problem of boredom. Only what you love never gets boring—until you stop loving it.

Only what gets old gets boring. And love never gets old. Love is always young, always new, always beginning.

What do we do when we practice the presence of the God who is infinite love? We do what love does and say what love says. We turn to him the four faces of love, which are the four themes of prayer:

Repentance

Adoration   *ACTS*

Petition

Thanksgiving

Repentance is an act of love. One of the most stupid and false lines in any movie in history is the famous line from *Love Story*: "Love means never having to say you're sorry." On the contrary, it is only love that says "I'm sorry." The Nazis never said they were sorry to the Jews.

Repentance is love also because it involves confession of wrong, and confession to God involves total trust in the love of the God we confess to. We are reluctant to confess our sins to those who we fear may stop loving us, who may misunderstand us and reject us for our sins because their understanding of us and their love for us are finite, flawed, and conditional. If you think about any person, "He will love me only if I perform well enough, only if I prove that I deserve his love, only if I am worthy", then you will fear to confess your unworthiness to that person. Only God will never stop loving us. Therefore we trust only God to confess our sins to.

Adoration is obviously love. "I adore you" are the words lovers speak. If spoken to a human being and meant literally, it is idolatry. Adoration lit-

erally means infinite love. It is to be given only to
the infinitely perfect, infinitely lovable being, God.
The Latin word for adoration is *latria*, as distinct
from *dulia*, which is finite, human love and respect. *Hyperdulia* is the highest, greatest finite and
human love and respect, which is to be given to
the greatest merely finite and human being who
ever lived, the Blessed Virgin Mary, the Mother of
God, who alone was sinless, "our tainted nature's
solitary boast".

Petition is the love of the things we ask for for
ourselves; and petition for others, or intercession,
is the love of those for whom we intercede.

Finally, thanksgiving is love's response to having been loved and for having been given the gifts
that express and incarnate love.

So the four themes of prayer are all themes of
love.

The four themes are easy to remember because
they make up the acronym RAPT (Repentance,
Adoration, Petition, Thanksgiving). We are not
only to pray but to be *rapt* in prayer, in rapturous
and self-forgetful love. We are also to be *wrapped*
in prayer; for prayer is not in us, we are in prayer.

RAPT is also the best order for these four
themes:

Beginning with repentance means that we come
into God's presence not casually or proudly but
humbly and honestly, through the only Way (Jn

14:6), the only Mediator (1 Tim 2:5), the One whose death tore open the curtain separating us from God's dwelling place, the "holy of holies" (Mt 27:50-51; Heb 10:19), giving us the access to God that our sins had prevented.

Once repentance has brought us into God's presence, the obvious and right thing to do is to adore. To see God is to adore him. Adoration is the heart of prayer. Most of the prayers in Scripture, especially the Psalms, are praise and adoration. Adoration should consume most of our time in prayer. Adoration has no limit, for its object (God) has no limit; the reasons for adoring the unlimited God are unlimited. In Heaven, our adoration will never end and never be bored. Of all earthly acts, adoration is the most heavenly.

Petition, like repentance, should usually be fairly short, for we have few needs, and God knows them better than we do. According to Christ's own prayer instructions, "Give us this day our daily bread" suffices for ourselves. But it does not suffice for others, that is, for intercession; and we should spend more time on our intercession for others than on our petitions for ourselves, not only out of charity but out of realism: because there *are* more others and therefore more needs.

Finally, it is good to end with thanksgiving because that can go on forever, like adoration, since we have an infinite number of gifts and blessings to thank God for, and as we mature we should learn to count to higher numbers. "Count your blessings" is not only good prayer and good honesty but also good therapy for depression, resentment, fear, doubt, and lovelessness.

9

"JESUS"

The Shortest, Simplest, and Most
Powerful Prayer in the World

I am now going to tell you about the shortest, simplest, and most powerful prayer in the world.

It is called the "Jesus Prayer", and it consists simply in uttering the single word "Jesus" (or "Lord Jesus", or "Lord Jesus Christ, have mercy on me, a sinner") in any situation, at any time and place, either aloud or silently.

There is only one prerequisite, one presupposition: that you are a Christian. If you have faith in Christ, hope in Christ, and love of Christ, you can pray the most powerful prayer in the world, because you have real contact with the greatest power in the universe: Christ himself, who assured us, in his last words to his apostles, that "All authority in heaven and on earth has been given to me" (Mt 28:18).

It is also the simplest of all prayers. It is not one of the many "methods", because it bypasses methods and cuts right to the heart of practicing God's

53

presence, which is the essence of prayer, the secret
of which has been given to us by God the Father.
The secret is simply God the Son, God incarnate,
the Lord Jesus.

Its simplicity and flexibility

As the *Catechism* says, "The invocation of the holy
name of Jesus is the simplest way of praying always. . . . This prayer is possible 'at all times' because it is not one occupation among others but
the only occupation: that of loving God, which
animates and transfigures every action in Christ
Jesus" (CCC 2668).

Because it is so short and simple, this prayer
can be prayed literally at any time at all and at all
times, even times when longer and more complex
forms of prayer are not practical or even possible.
This includes times of anguish, pain, or stress, and
times of deep happiness and joy.

It can be used by everyone (and has been): by
the rankest beginner and the most advanced saint.
It is not only for beginners; the saints use it too.
It is not "cheating" just because it is so short. For
it will make you pray more, not less. This only
sounds paradoxical, for one of the things Jesus re-
minds us to do, when we invoke him by name, is
to pray more!

It is so simple that it is like the center point of

a circle. It is the whole circle. It contains in itself the whole gospel. The *Catechism* says: "The name 'Jesus' contains all: God and man and the whole economy of creation and salvation" (CCC 2666). Into this name the Christian can pour all of his faith, with nothing whatsoever left over, for to be a Christian is to rest all of your faith on Christ, with nothing left over.

It is not only the shortest *prayer* but also the shortest and earliest *creed*. Twice the New Testament mentions this most basic of all the Christian creeds: the simple three-word sentence "Jesus is Lord" (1 Cor 12:3) and the same creed in four words: "Jesus Christ is Lord" (Phil 2:11). It is also the most distinctively Christian creed, for "Lord" (*Kyrios*) means "God", and Christ's divinity and lordship over one's life is the distinctive, essential faith of Christians: no non-Christian believes that (if he did, he would be a Christian), and all Christians believe it (if they do not, they are not Christians).

What it is not: Magic

Like any prayer, it "works", not by the power of some impersonal magic but by the power of personal faith and hope and love. It is like a sacrament in that way: it "works" objectively (*ex opere operato*), by the power of God's action, not ours;

but it does not "work" without our free choice.
It is like turning on a hose: the water comes *to* us,
not *from* us, but it comes only when we choose to
let it through.

The mere pronunciation of the name "Jesus"
is not *invoking* him and is not prayer. A parrot
could do that. God does not deal in magic, because
magic bypasses the soul, especially the heart; it is
like a machine. But God is a lover, and he wants
our hearts, wants to transform our hearts, wants
to live in our hearts.

Love is its own end. Magic, like technology, is
always used as a means to some greater end. If you
pray this prayer as a means, as a kind of magic or
spiritual technology, then you are using it as you
would use a machine or magic spell. What you
love and desire is the higher end, the thing that
the machine or magic spell gets you. But whatever that thing is, the love of *things*—of God's
gifts instead of God—does not bring God closer;
it pushes him farther away. So using this prayer as
a kind of magic does exactly the opposite of what
prayer is supposed to do.

When you pray this prayer, do not concentrate
on the name, the word, the sound, or the letters.
Do not think of the name but of Jesus. And do
not try to meditate on scenes from the Gospels or
truths from theology, or to imagine what Jesus
looks like, as you do in some other forms of
prayer. Just reach out to Jesus in blind faith. "The

principal thing is to stand before God with the mind in the heart, and to go on standing before Him unceasingly day and night, until the end of life" (Bishop Theophan, quoted by Kallistos Ware in *The Power of the Name: The Jesus Prayer in Orthodox Spirituality*).

What it is not: Psychology

This prayer is not merely subjective, like a psychological device, any more than it is merely objective, like magic. It is not a sort of Christian yoga. It is not meditation. Its purpose is not to transform our consciousness and make us mystics, or to bring inner peace, or to center on our own heart. Whether these things are good or bad, these things are not what this prayer is for.

For all these things are subjective, inside the human soul; but this prayer is dialogue, relationship, reaching out to another person, to Jesus, God made man, invoking him as your savior, lover, lord, and God. You have faith and hope in him as your savior; you love him as your lover; you obey him as your lord; you adore him as your God.

In this prayer our attention is not directed inward, into our own consciousness, but only out onto Jesus. Even when we address Jesus living in our own soul, he is not self but other; he is Lord of the self.

Yet, although our intention in this prayer is not

to transform our consciousness, this prayer *does* transform our consciousness. How? It unifies it. Our usual consciousness is like an unruly, stormy sea, or like a flock of chattering monkeys, or a cage of butterflies, or a hundred little bouncing balls of mercury spilled from a fever thermometer. We cannot gather it together. Only God can, for God is the *Logos*. One of the meanings of this incredibly rich word in ancient Greek, the word given to the eternal, divine, pre-incarnate Christ, is "gathering-into-one". When we pray this prayer and invoke Jesus the Logos, Jesus the Logos acts and does in fact unify our consciousness. But this is not what we aim at; we aim at *him*. The unification of our consciousness happens in us (slowly and subtly and sweetly) only when we forget ourselves in him. This is one of the ways "he who loses his self shall find it."

Repetition of the holy name conditions our unconscious mind to see this name as normal, as central, and to *expect* him to be present and active, as a dog is conditioned by his master to see its master as central and to expect its master to be present and active. Do we train our dogs but not our own unconscious minds?

You may object, "But this sounds like a magic spell or a mantra: something not rational." In a sense it is (though not in the sense repudiated above). Do you not know that black magic can

be overcome only by white magic, not by reason? *Jesus*
And our culture's secularism and materialism is a *abnormal*
powerful spell of black magic. It makes us judge
Jesus by its standards instead of judging it by his
standards, because it makes us see Jesus as abnormal and our culture as normal; to see Jesus as a
questionable, tiny thing surrounded by an unques-
tionable, greater thing, namely, our culture. This is
a cosmic illusion! Invoking the holy name builds
up resistance to that illusion. That is not black
magic; it is not itself an illusion but sheer realism. Jesus IS everywhere and everywhen and the
ultimate meaning of everything. This prayer indeed conditions us, but it conditions us to know
reality.

What it is: Power

"The kingdom of God does not consist in talk but
in power", says Saint Paul (1 Cor 4:20). The reason this prayer is so powerful is that the name of
Jesus is not just a set of letters or sounds. It is not
a passive word but a creative word, like the word
by which God created the universe. (He *is* the
Word by which God created the universe!) Every
time we receive Christ in the Eucharist, we are
instructed by the liturgy to pray, "Lord, I am not
worthy to receive you, *but only say the word* and I
shall be healed." All our energy and effort is not

strong enough to heal our own souls, but God's
word of power is. That word is so powerful that
by it God made the universe out of nothing, and
by it he is doing the even greater deed of making
saints out of sinners. That word is Jesus Christ.

In most ancient societies, a person's name was
treated, not as a mere artificial label for pragmatic
purposes of human communication, but as a truth,
a sign of the person's unique identity. Revealing
your name was thus an act of intimate personal
trust, like a handshake. A handshake originally
meant: "See? I bear no weapon. You can trust
me." It is a little like your P.I.N. today.

In all of human history, God revealed his own
true name, his eternal name, only to one man—
Moses—and only to one people—the Hebrews,
his own "chosen people"—and only at one time
—at the burning bush (Ex 3). This name was the
secret no philosopher or mystic had ever attained,
the very essence of God, the nature of ultimate
reality: "I AM."

But then, many centuries later, God did an even
greater thing; he revealed a new name in Jesus
("Savior"). This is now the most precious name
in the world.

It is a golden key. It opens all doors, transforms
all corners of our lives. But we do not use this
golden key, and doors remain locked. In fact, our
society is dying because it has turned the most

precious name in the world, the name of its Savior, into a casual curse word.

Even Muslims respect the holy name of Jesus more than Christians do, in practice: they commonly add "blessed be he" every time they pronounce it.

In the Acts of the Apostles (3:1−10), Peter and John heal a man lame from birth when they say, "In the name of Jesus Christ, walk." Throughout the history of the Church and the lives of the saints, many such miracles of healing have been done "in his name". Exorcisms are performed "in his name". The name of Jesus is so powerful that it can knock the devil out of a soul!

The name of Jesus is our salvation. John ends his Gospel with this summary: "These [things] are written that you may believe that Jesus is the Christ, the Son of God, and that believing you may have life *in his name*" (Jn 20:31, emphasis added). "The name of Jesus Christ" is not only the key to power-filled prayer but the key to our salvation. So we had better understand it! What does the phrase "in the name of Jesus Christ" mean?

Suppose you are poor, but your father is rich. When you try to cash a check for half a million dollars in your own name, you will get only a laugh from the bank. But if the check is in your father's name, you will get the money. Our

Father in Heaven gave us unlimited grace in the "account" of Jesus Christ and then put us "into Christ", inserted us into his family, so that we can use the family name, so to speak, to cash checks on the account of divine grace. Saint Paul tells us that our account is unlimited: "My God will supply every need of yours according to his riches in glory in Christ Jesus" (Phil 4:19). Jesus himself first assured us of this wonderful truth, which we find hard to believe because it seems too good to be true, and then he explained why it *is* true:

> Ask, and it will be given you; seek, and you will find; knock, and it will be opened to you. For every one who asks receives, and he who seeks finds, and to him who knocks it will be opened. What man of you, if his son asks him for bread, will give him a stone? Or if he asks for a fish, will give him a serpent? If you then, who are evil, know how to give good gifts to your children, how much more will your Father who is in heaven give good things to those who ask him! (Mt 7:7–11).

If even we love our children so much that we do not settle for anything less than the very best for them, why do we think God loves his children less?

What it is: Real presence

It is probably a very good exercise to practice "the imitation of Christ", to walk "in his steps", to ask "What would Jesus do?" in all circumstances. But the prayer we are teaching now is even better, for two reasons. First, invoking his name invokes his real presence, not mental imitation; something objective, not subjective; between us and him, not just in us. Second, it is actual, not potential; indicative, not subjunctive; "What is Jesus doing?" rather than "What would Jesus do?"

To invoke Jesus' name is to place yourself in his presence, to open yourself to his power, his energy. The prayer of Jesus' name actually brings God closer, makes him more present. He is always present in some way, since he knows and loves each one of us at every moment; but he is not present to those who do not pray as intimately as he is present to those who do. Prayer makes a difference; "prayer changes things." It may or may not change our external circumstances. (It does if God sees that that change is good for us; it does not if God sees that it is not.) But it always changes our relationship to God, which is infinitely more important than external circumstances, however pressing they may seem, because it is eternal but they are temporary, and because it is our very self but they are not.

What it is: Grace

In saying it brings God closer, I do not mean to say that it changes God. It changes us. But it does not just make a change within us, a psychological change; it makes a change *between* us and God, a real, objective change. It changes the real relationship; it increases the intimacy. It is as real as changing your relationship to the sun by going outdoors. When we go outdoors into the sun, we do not move the sun closer to us, we move ourselves closer to the sun. But the difference it makes is real: we can get warmed only when we stand in the sunlight—and in the Sonlight.

When this happens, it is not merely something we do but something God does in us. It is grace, it is his action; our action is to enter into his action, as a tiny stream flows into a great river.

His coming is, of course, his gift, his grace. The vehicle by which he comes is also his grace: it is Jesus himself. And the gift he gives us in giving us his blessed name to invoke is also his grace. So, therefore, his coming to us in power on this vehicle, this name, is also pure grace. Even our remembering to use this vehicle, this name, is his grace. As Saint Thérèse said, "Everything is a grace."

What it is: Sacramental

The *Catechism* says: "To pray 'Jesus' is to invoke him and to call him within us. His name is the only one that contains the presence it signifies" (CCC 2666). In other words, it is sacramental.

God comes to us on his name like a king on his stallion. When we pray to the Father in Jesus' name, we provide God with a vehicle to come to us—or, rather, we use the vehicle God has provided for us. We do not initiate, we respond; we respond to his grace by using the gift of his name that he gave us and told us to use; and he responds to our obedience by doing what he promised: actually coming.

This is the definition of a sacrament: a sign instituted by Christ to give grace and a sign that actually *effects* what it *signifies*. Jesus himself is the primary sacrament. So the believing Christian's use of Jesus' name is sacramental. The very act of praying "Jesus" effects what it signifies, brings about what the name "Jesus" signifies, which is "Savior", or "God saves". That is the literal meaning, in Hebrew, of the name God commanded Joseph to give to Mary's son: "You shall call his name Jesus, for he will save his people from their sins" (Mt 1:21).

A *name* is not a *machine*, for a *person* is not a machine. The name of a person must be personally "invoked" (that is, called upon) in faith and hope and love, as a human father is "invoked" by his son in Jesus' parable in Matthew 7. But though it is not a machine, it really "works": when a son calls to his father, "Dad!" the father actually comes. Why? Suppose we were to ask the father. His answer would be obvious: "Because that's my son!" The same is true of our relationship to God now that Christ has made us God's children and his brothers. No stranger can call a human being "Dad", and no stranger can be sure that a man will come if he calls him only by his "proper name", for example, "Mr. Smith". But Mr. Smith's son can be sure his dad will come because his son can invoke him under the name "Dad", as no one else can. Jesus has made it possible for us to do the same with God. In fact, the name he taught us to call God is "Abba", which is the Hebrew word, not just for "Father", but for "Dad", or "Daddy", or even "Dada". It is the word of ultimate intimacy.

You may think the claim that invoking his name actually brings about his presence is an arrogant one. But in fact it is a humble one, because it is obeying his design, not initiating our own.

Or you may think, "What right do we have to think he will come whenever we call? Is he a dog?" No, he is a lover.

What it is: Sacred

The fact that this holy name of Jesus actually
brings about the presence of God explains why
God gave us, as the second of all his command-
ments, "You shall not take the name of the LORD
your God in vain" (Ex 20:7). In the Old Testament, the self-revealed name of God was YHWH,
in Hebrew: a name always written without the
vowels because it was forbidden to pronounce it,
since it meant "I AM", or "I AM WHO AM", and
to pronounce that name is to claim to bear it.
You can pronounce any other name, like "Ivan"
or "Mary" or "Hey, You" without claiming to be
the person who bears that name; there is only one
name that you cannot say in the second person
(you) or the third person (he or she), and that is
"I". Thus no Jew ever dared to pronounce that
holy name, or even guess how the vowels were
supposed to be pronounced, because it could be
truly spoken only by God himself. That is why the
Jews tried to execute Jesus for blasphemy when he
pronounced it in his own name (Jn 8:58).

And that is also why Jesus commanded us to
pray to the Father, as the very first petition of
the model prayer he taught (which we call the
Lord's Prayer, or the Our Father) "Hallowed be
thy name" (Mt 6:9). For we actually bring about
and fulfill what we pray for when we call on the

holy name of Jesus. We bring his presence and his
mercy down from Heaven to earth, so to speak.
Thus it is blasphemy to treat this holy name like
any other name, because it has a holy power un-
like any other power.

Its practice

I will tell you a little bit from my own experience
about what I think will happen when you use this
prayer. For I have tried many other, more complex, and more abstract ways to pray, and I have
found them all less effective than this most child-
like of all ways.

Perhaps the most shattering consequence of his
real presence, which is brought about by invoking his name, is that we become unable to lie to
ourselves any more. He is light, and wherever he
inserts his lordship there is now an absolute necessity of honesty and a zero tolerance for any
form of self-deception, self-congratulation, or self-
gratification, even those forms that felt necessary,
natural, and almost innocent before. He is gentle,
but he is light, and he simply does not and will
not coexist with any darkness at all; either he casts
it out, or it keeps him out.

This is the negative dimension of the fact that
he is light. He subtracts our falsehoods. But he
also adds his truth. The positive dimension is es-

sentially a clarification of vision, of perspective, of "the big picture". He does not (usually) give specific directions or instant solutions, but he always gives a clarification of our vision. (This usually happens gradually.)

Thus there is a positive side to even the negative point made above. For instance, he makes us men see how flawed and mixed our motives are even in such natural and spontaneous things as a look into the face of a beautiful woman. (Half of all the women in the world are beautiful to men, nearly all are beautiful when they smile, and all are beautiful all the time to God.) We find that there is something in this look that is his, and also something that is not from him but is from the world, the flesh, or the Enemy.

And yet this insight does not bring about a guilty despair but a happy humility. For it is a sign of his presence. He is the standard. When the plumb line is present, apparently straight lines show their inclination. And this is, of course, upsetting (how easily our lines incline!), but much more is it a cause of joy (it is he!). As John Wesley said, "The best thing is, God is with us." Once we realize that, we have the secret of joy: simply to do all that is from his will with joy, because he is there, and what is not from his will do not do.

And when his light and our darkness, his straight and our crooked, are thus brought into relationship and warfare, we gain rather than lose, even if it is upsetting. It is like bringing in the Roto-Rooter man: the garbage becomes visible, but it also becomes removable. Before his light came in, our sin was just as much present but undetected. But he was not just as much present. So that is a gain. Furthermore, he is stronger than sin; he exorcises sin more than sin exorcises him. All we have to do is to give him a chance. Open the blinds, and light casts out darkness every time.

This new sense of vision or perspective that invoking his name brings about is most sharply perceived when we invoke his name upon our problems and complaints. The wordless message I seem to get most frequently is something like this: "There are things that are infinitely more important for you than these little problems. They are all little compared to me. In fact, most of what you think of as your problems are in fact your opportunities—opportunities for the really important thing, the 'one thing needful', your relationship with me. So get on with it. You don't have much more time." He is surprisingly brisk and unsentimental. He is a no-nonsense God.

Perhaps the most definite and ubiquitous sign of his real presence, and the clearest difference between the times when I invoke his name and the times when I do not, is the state of quiet, calm alertness that he brings. Usually, I am either calm or alert, not both. When I am calm, I am relaxed and ready for sleep; when I am alert, I am worried or agitated and ready for problems. His peace, however, is not sleepiness, and his alertness is not anxiety.

His presence manifests itself, not in fire or wind or thunder, but in a still, small voice. Only in this quietness does he give us the certainty of his presence. We usually cannot hear this because we are making so much inner noise, especially when we are agitated. But this is when he wants most to come, for he goes where the need is.

And what happens when we invoke him during our agitation? He answers! But not by magic or spectacle. Nothing spectacular happens when I invoke the holy name at times when I am reacting to my problems by the "fight-or-flight response" that is so natural to our animal nature (that is, either by the "fight" of inner rage and resentment or by the "flight" of self-pity and fantasizing). At such times, when I pray his name, I do not suddenly feel holy or happy, but I do suddenly feel . . . well, "mature" is the only word that comes to mind. The word from the Word is often something like "Grow up!" I suddenly see that far more *important* things are at stake than my feelings, when I let his great wave come in and wash my little garbage away. What had looked big on my beach looks tiny in his waves.

We do not always get specific answers, even
when we invoke his name; but we always get the
Answerer. It is better to have his authority for
"no answer" than our authority for ours. When
I am in the middle of some garbage, he gives me
no answer to my questions "*Why* did you put me
here?" or "*How* do I solve it?", but he gives me instead an answer to another question: "*Who?*" It is
he. That is his answer: himself. The real question
is: "*Who's there?*" And the answer is in Matthew
14:27.

We always start our sentences with "I". We
unconsciously play God. He teaches us to see our
"I" as surrounded by him instead of vice versa.
He is no longer an ingredient in our experience;
we are ingredients in his. We are actors in his
play; he is not an actor in ours, not even the most
important actor.

Let me give you a small example of the positive side to this "sense of perspective" that we
get from invoking his name. The other day he re-
minded me to speak his name while I was painting an unimportant piece of porch wood, and I
suddenly saw that what I was doing was not just
painting a porch but painting a portrait, myself; I
was walking Home to him. Each brush stroke was
a small step to Heaven. Heaven was here in this
old porch, too. For all beauty, even this tiny bit
of it that I was making, is his, is like him; beauty
is one of the things he is, and all earthly beauty

is a sunbeam of his sun. I remembered the story of two men hauling stones through a muddy medieval street. One was cursing and the other was singing. A traveler asked them what they were doing. The curser replied, "I'm trying to get this damned rock to roll through this damned mud!" The singer replied, "I'm building a cathedral."

Is there any downside to this prayer? What is the main problem with this prayer?

Simply remembering to do it. This is embarrassing, because this forgetting is so foolish. Why do we forget? Clearly this forgetting is not merely a mental problem. There are mental blocks to remembering. Something in us *fears* remembering. And I think we all know what that is.

When we do remember and call him, and he comes and acts, he does all the work, for free! Our part is only to call; the Great Physician makes house calls and charges nothing. And yet we continually fail to call him. Is this reasonable?

The solution to this "forgetting" is not in our power but his. In order to receive, we must ask for the grace of remembering to ask. And for the grace to trust him with our thoughts as well as with our lives. He is the Master also of our miserable memories. A thought comes into our mind when *he* says, "Come!" and leaves when *he* says "Go!" He is the centurion, our thoughts are his soldiers. The Lord giveth, the Lord taketh away, blessed be the name of the Lord.

10

WORK

Praying Always

We are commanded to "pray constantly" (1 Thess 5:17). But most of our life is filled with actions. Therefore our actions can also be a form of prayer. Brother Lawrence says, "We are as strictly obliged to adhere to God by action in the time of action as by prayer in the time of prayer" (Conversation 4). The practice of the presence of God, though we begin it at special times of prayer, is designed to spill out and over and into all times.

God designed us to be animals (rational animals), not angels. He put us into a material world, and he put into our nature the need for many kinds of material actions, such as eating, sleeping, begetting, and working. He could not possibly have designed these things to be distractions and obstacles to our sanctification, but only means to it, for he designed everything to be a means to that end. Therefore we can pray even *in* working (not just *as* we work); we can make our works prayers.

How do we make our works prayer? Not by

changing our work (unless our work is sinful or shoddy or dishonest or lazy), but by changing our motive. Instead of peeling potatoes because we want to taste them, we peel them because we love God, the God who wants us to peel potatoes right now. Brother Lawrence says to "pick up a straw for the love of God" (Conversation 2). Mother Teresa said, "Some theologians talk too much. They should pick up a broom and sweep the room. That says enough."

God designed us to reach holiness in and through doing little things, such as cleaning up a room, driving children to soccer, balancing the checkbook, or peeling potatoes. These times are holy, too, and these times are his, too. He does not want only our "quality time" (a fake and dishonest phrase if there ever was one; ask any child); he wants all our time, for the same reason he does not want only part of our heart but our whole heart: because he is our Lover, not our boss.

He wants our work time as well as our "prayer time" because he designed work as well as prayer for us, and he designed them both for the same reason. As Pascal says, "God instituted prayer in order to impart to us his creatures the dignity of being causes" (*Pensées*).

He put us into a world full of "little things", so we must conclude that they are the road he designed for us to come to him and he to us, and

[margin handwritten note: Terese of Lisieux]

therefore they are big things. He says this himself, in a warning whose seriousness we seldom notice: "He who is faithful in a very little is faithful also in much; and he who is dishonest in a very little is dishonest also in much. If then you have not been faithful in the unrighteous mammon, who will entrust to you the true riches?" (Lk 16:10–11).

11

DISTRACTIONS

Mental Obstacles to Prayer

Whoever you are, I guarantee that one thing will certainly happen to you if you seriously try to practice the presence of God as this book suggests: you will fail. You will fail over and over again. Unless you are better than the saints.

The saints, too, had wandering minds. The saints, too, had constantly to recall their constantly wandering mind-child home. They became saints because they continued to go after the little wanderer, like the Good Shepherd.

Here is what will happen when you begin to pray in earnest. You will begin to focus your attention on God alone when you pray, and this will give you a deep peace and a deep joy and a deep sense of *rightness*; yet after a very little while you will find, to your dismay, that you have not been focusing your attention on God at all for quite some time! As soon as you turned your back on your mind, it ran away from peace and joy and rightness and started fantasizing, or falling asleep, or worrying about other things.

You are dismayed at this. Good. This dismay means that it happened against your will. You did not *want* to stop focusing on God; you wanted just the opposite. But "the spirit indeed is willing, but the flesh is weak" (Mt 26:41).

(By the way, "spirit" and "flesh" in the New Testament do *not* mean "soul" and "body". There are four separate Greek words for them [*pneuma*, *sarx*, *psyche*, and *soma*]. "Spirit" is the whole self as redeemed and directed by the Holy Spirit; "flesh" is the whole self as fallen and selfish.)

We should be dismayed but not surprised at this weakness. We should *expect* our minds to wander like lawless infants. If we are surprised at this habitual slide away from God, that may be a more serious problem than the slide, because that is pride.

God is infinitely patient and understanding with our weaknesses, and we should be patient, too. We get in as much trouble when we are impatient with God's patience as we do when we are impatient with God's impatience. God is patient with us because what is precious to him is not our achievements but our intentions, our will, our heart. As Mother Teresa loved to say, God does not demand that we be successful; God demands that we be faithful.

The problem of distractions in prayer is universal, and many books waste much too much attention on it, thus making the problem another problem and another distraction—from God and from loving him. The best "method" of dealing with distractions is no method at all. Once you discover that you have been out of his presence, simply go back. Do not berate yourself. Do not give excuses. Do not plan how to avoid it next time. Do not think about yourself or about your distractions at all. Do not give them the attention they do not deserve. They are like a million little gnats that keep buzzing around your head whatever you do. You cannot kill them with a direct attack, as you can kill one big bug with a stroke of a swatter. So don't try. Just ignore them and turn to the business at hand—prayer—again and again. Do it a million times if necessary. Get right back on the horse every time you fall off.

Suppose you were doing something very important and difficult that required concentration, such as driving a school bus full of children down a fast highway through heavy traffic. If a swarm of gnats surrounded your head and you could not get rid of them or stop the bus, you would have only two choices: you could pay attention to the gnats and swat at them, thus risking losing control of the bus; or you could pay attention to your job as bus driver and get the children safely out of traffic and to the school, whether one or a million gnats came at you.

All other methods for dealing with distractions, anything more complex than repeating the name of Jesus in faith, will probably do the opposite of what they are designed to do, because they call attention to the distractions, or to themselves as methods for dealing with the distractions. Just turn away from distractions. Don't give them the time of day.

But "don't think about them" can be self-defeating. Consider the command, "Don't think of a blue monkey!" It calls attention to the very thing it commands you to deflect attention away from. If you want to avoid thinking about a blue monkey, you have to think about a red rhinoceros. Saint Thomas Aquinas says, wisely, that the only way to drive out a bad passion is by a stronger good passion. The same is true of thoughts as of passions.

When your mind wanders, like a child, your *will* must bring it back, like a mother. (I mean by "the will", not "willpower" or "strength of will", but simply "choice" or "decision" or "resolution"). The will-parent must discipline the mind-child, avoiding both the opposite extremes commonly made in disciplining either children or thoughts: tyranny or permissiveness. The will must be to the mind what God is to us, namely, "easy to please but hard to satisfy". The good parent is pleased at the infant's first stumbling steps but will not be satisfied with anything short of a runner's grace.

To review, the only three salient points about distractions are these: First, we must expect them and be patient with ourselves. Second, we must simply ignore them and "get back on the horse" over and over again. And third, it is the will that gets the mind back on the horse.

12

SINS

Moral Obstacles to Prayer

When we find in ourselves not just laziness but a fear or aversion to prayer, that is usually caused by something more than mental distractions. To find its cause, ask yourself: What in me is repelled by God, afraid of his presence? Which cells in the body hate the good surgeon? Cancer cells. What is there in me that finds God its enemy? Only one thing: sin.

Failure in the will—sin—is a much more radical failure, and a greater obstacle to prayer, than failure in the mind—distractions—and the solution therefore has to be much more radical. In fact, the solution is beyond human power. That is the bad news. The good news is that God has provided that solution: forgiveness for all our sins through the blood of Jesus Christ. That is basic Christianity; that is the gospel.

There are two parts to the forgiveness of sins: God's giving it and our receiving it. Forgiveness is a gift, and like any gift it must be both freely given and freely received. God always gives it. But we do not always receive it. Our receiving it is dependent on our (1) repentance, (2) confession, and (3) faith.

Why are these three things necessary? Because if I offer you a pardon, you will not get it if (1) you do not want it, or if (2) you do not think you need it, or if (3) you do not trust me enough to accept it. Similarly with God's pardon of our sins: we will not receive it if (1) we want to sin instead of wanting to turn away from sin and turn to God (which is what "repentance" means); or if (2) we do not admit that we need it (which is what "confession" means); or if (3) we do not trust in the One who gives it (which is what "faith" means). God never closes his hand, but we sometimes close ours.

One way we close our hand to receiving his forgiveness is by closing our hand to giving forgiveness to others. This is so dangerous that Christ, in giving us the Lord's Prayer, commanded us to pray for our own damnation if we do not forgive all who sin against us: "Forgive us our trespasses *as we forgive those who trespass against us.*"

We must turn from sin in order to turn to prayer. Sin inhibits prayer as infidelity inhibits love. Prayer seeks God's presence, while sin turns away from God's presence. We must turn from sin in order to pray, just as we must turn from prayer in order to sin. For prayer is the practice of the presence of God, and sin cannot endure God's presence, as a vampire cannot endure the sunlight. So the habit of prayer is our strongest protection against sin. Sin and prayer are opposites; they are darkness and light.

Repentance, confession, and faith do not *add* to God's forgiveness; they let it in. God's forgiveness is not *dependent* on our repentance, confession, and faith; it is dependent on Christ's blood. Christ's blood is more than adequate for all sins. Once you have repented, confessed, and believed, you have received God's forgiveness in full, and if you think you are too great a sinner for Christ's blood to be sufficient for full forgiveness, you are insulting not yourself but God, for you are telling the Great Physician that his medicine is not strong enough and that you have to add to it by concocting some of your own. The medicine is his own blood, and it cannot be made stronger, only weaker. Our part is simply to receive it and believe it. The penances we do, we do *because* we have been forgiven, not *in order to be* forgiven.

If you think you are too great a sinner to approach God in prayer; if you are still weighed down and worried about your sins even though you have believed and been baptized (and thus received Christ) and even though you have made a sincere confession (and thus received Christ's forgiveness for your sins), then I will tell you what kind of fool you are. You are like the fool who was walking to market carrying a donkey on his back. A farmer with a horse and cart saw him and said, "You fool! You'll break your back that way! Climb on my cart and I'll give you a ride to market." So the fool climbed on the cart. But when they arrived at the market, the farmer saw that the fool had broken his back anyway, because even when he had climbed aboard the cart, he had never taken the donkey off his back.

Once you receive God's forgiveness of your sins, they *are* forgiven—unless he is a liar. God says that you are clean and restored to the Father's family like the prodigal son, not because you are good enough, but because Christ is good enough. God says it, you believe it, and that settles it. Brother Lawrence says, "we ought, *without anxiety*, to *expect* the pardon of our sins from the blood of Jesus Christ" (Conversation 1; emphasis added). That simple faith in Christ's blood is a more effective deterrent to our committing future sins than any haunting sense of guilt and anxiety about our weakness and unworthiness.

Of course we are weak and unworthy! But we must not get ingrown eyeballs. We must keep our eyes on Christ, not on ourselves. Our selves are like our eyes: designed for looking outward. God gave us our eyes to see, our ears to hear, and our hands to help, not themselves but others. The human self is remarkably inept at helping itself. Leave that little worm in God's hands; it is far too slippery for you to handle.

13

SIMPLICITY

Prayer as Saint-Making

In the last chapter, we turned from the mind to the will in turning from the problem of distractions to the problem of sins. For the rest of the book, we will explore this deeper problem of taming the will, for that is the key to becoming saints, that is, to becoming our true selves, becoming what God designed us to be. That is the ultimate purpose of prayer. Prayer does not exist for its own sake; it exists to transform us into saints.

Sanctity is both hard and simple, and for the same reason. It is hard *because* it is so simple; for it is the state of simplicity, or singleness, or purity of heart (Mt 5:8). (In scriptural language, "heart" means "will", not "feelings".) "Purity of heart is to will [that is, to love] one thing", says Kierkegaard. That one thing is God, and what God is: goodness. So sanctity is very easy to understand: it means simply loving God with all your heart, obeying what Jesus called "the great and first commandment" (Mt 22:38). And it is hard to attain for the same reason it is easy to understand: its simplicity. What makes it hard is the "all" in "love God with all your heart."

It is not hard to *understand* that God deserves all our love, since he is the source of all our good, beginning with our very existence. But it is hard to *give* him all our love.

Almost anyone can love God partially. A saint loves God totally. Anyone can love God as *a* god; a saint loves God as God.

Sanctity is like dieting. We are far too fat (spiritually). The man whom Jesus called the greatest of all the prophets, John the Baptist, gave us the formula for sanctity: "He must increase, but I must decrease" (Jn 3:30). We are far too full of ourselves to be able to be filled with God. God can fill only "the hungry" with good things, while "the rich" he can only send away empty (Lk 1:53)—not because he withholds his love from the rich (those who are filled with themselves), but because the rich have no room for him—like the inn in Bethlehem.

What do we do when we are too fat? We diet. What do we do when we are too rich? We give our riches away. What do we do when we are too burdened to be good soldiers? We get rid of our burdens, like Gideon (Judg 7). We must pour ourselves out for the love of God.

What do these metaphors mean, literally and

concretely? Brother Lawrence answers: "Our sanctification does not depend upon changing our works, but in doing that for God's sake which we commonly do for our own. It is lamentable to see how many people mistake the means for the end, addicting themselves to certain works" (Conversation 4).

The only works we all have to change in order to become saints are sins. What we have to change is our heart, our desire, our love, our intentions. We must do everything for God, even picking up a straw. We must, in the words of the "morning offering" prayer, offer it up—offer *everything*, all our "prayers, works, joys, and sufferings". And we must continue this "morning offering" right through till evening and till death.

God provides not only abstract instructions but also concrete examples. Our perfect example and model here is Mary. Her simplicity is so perfect that it reduces her to a single word: *fiat*, "let it be to me according to your word" (Lk 1:38). This *fiat* is the word of power that God spoke to bring the universe into existence out of nothing (Gen 1). When Mary spoke it, God worked an even greater miracle: he made himself man. God longs for us to speak it a third time, so that the greatest miracle of all can happen: a saint can be made out of a sinner. This is an even greater miracle because God encountered no resistance from the nothingness out of which he made the universe or from the sinless perfection of the Blessed Virgin Mary out of which he made his incarnate humanity; but he encounters the resistance of sin in us. Nevertheless, he will not rest until he has made a perfect saint out of this resistant and recalcitrant sinner.

Mary's heart is like the point of a sword. Her whole self comes to this point. All in her is *fiat*, nothing else. She does not need to add anything to that; any addition would be a subtraction. That is why Scripture says so little about her and why she speaks so few words. She did not need to preach a sermon, or write a book, or start a school.

Becoming so simple and Mary-like is a lifelong process, of course, and for most of us probably much longer, to be completed only in Purgatory, where the sword of our spirit will be hammered into a perfect point. (That is why the pains of Purgatory are more joyful than the greatest joys on earth.)

This goal of perfection and simplicity is not an option for the elite few; it is the prerequisite for Heaven. Nothing impure can enter Heaven. We are in for the full treatment. God is not a compromiser, because God is perfect love. The only alternative is Hell. He will have his way with us, whether the short and easy way or the long and hard way. We *must* be perfect, as our Father is perfect (Mt 5:48). That is not a man's decree but God's, and therefore it is nonnegotiable.

The reason for this nonnegotiable demand is also nonnegotiable: it is God's own eternal nature. God is perfect love, and perfect love demands the perfection of the beloved. Only imperfect love can be satisfied with the beloved still in parts and tatters. Perfect love alone treats the beloved as a whole, a unity; perfect love alone knows the beloved because it penetrates to the single "I" beneath all the many qualities and acts.

Perfect love is also altruistic, not egotistic. It is for our sake, not his, that God is such a perfectionist. He does not need us at all, but we need him totally. He insists on possessing us totally because he knows we need to possess him totally, even if we do not know that yet. And that is why he will burn away all our fat until we are empty enough to be filled with his fatness (Ps 63:5; 65:11), his fullness.

Even earthly lovers, if they are not cold and calculating but passionate, want nothing less than to be wholly united with their beloved. They set no limits, make no deals, accept no compromises, and burn all their bridges behind them for love. It is "all or nothing"—that is, if they are true lovers. How can God be and do any less?

To be thus swallowed up by love, to become wholly God's, to lose all our spiritual fat, is to become what we truly are, to achieve our true identity, the identity we had in the mind of our Creator when he designed us. How could the true identity of the creature, all of whose being and truth come from its Creator, possibly be found anywhere else? There *is* nowhere else. God is not *a* god; God is God, the source of all being and all truth.

This goal is not only the perfection of *sanctity*, it is also the perfection of *sanity*, of right-reality-response, of living in objective reality instead of in our subjective fantasies. For in reality, we *are* wholly God's. We are *creatures*: our very act of existence is not our own but his gift, on permanent loan. We are nothing in ourselves because he created us out of nothing. If he had formed us out of something, then that something, that raw material, would be ours, though the form would be his. But there is nothing in us that is not his, for the "nothing" out of which he created us is simply nothing.

We are already wholly his by right, but because of sin we are not yet wholly his in fact because we do not wholly will what we are by right. We are thus not wholly what we are: we are not in fact what we are by right. Our very being is broken into these two parts, fact and right, like a broken stick. We must be healed, wholed, in our very being. This is the "one thing . . . needful" (Lk 10:42); this is our "categorical imperative". We must become in fact what we are by right: we must become wholly God's.

This is why prayer is so important: it sets us firmly on that road. Prayer is essentially the practice of the presence of God, and that is the road to Heaven. There is no alternative. God is the only game in town. All other roads are dead ends.

Since we must give our all to the one true God, we must not give any part to idols, to the many false gods that now bite away at our lives. Thus there is a negative side to "the first and greatest commandment". That we must love God with *all* our heart means that we must *not* love any other god with *any* of our heart.

This does not mean that we must not love God's creatures, God's material creations. But we must love them as he commands, not as we command; as his gifts, not as things in themselves; in other words, as they are, not as we imagine them to be. And it certainly does not mean that we should not love his *human* creatures, our brothers and sisters, his children. But it means that we must love them as they are: as our equals, our brothers and sisters, not as our gods. They are not our God, and things are not our God, and we are not our own God; only God is God. We must be as clear as Muslims, who wisely remind themselves five times a day that "there is no god but God" (*La ilaha illa'Llah*). That *theology* must become our *morality*.

14

RENUNCIATION

The Necessity of the Negative

We need to explore the negative side of sanctity more, because this is what gives us the most trouble, both to understand and to accept, and to practice and achieve. There is a single word for it: "renunciation". It means "refusing", or "saying No to", or "turning away from", or "turning our back on". What does this mean?

First, of course, it means renouncing sin, turning absolutely away from any and all sins, that is, every thought or word or deed or omission that is contrary to God's will.

But that is just the beginning. There is more. Renouncing sin means renouncing everything we are aware leads *away* from God. But we are also called to renounce everything we are aware does *not* lead to God: things innocent in themselves but that function as distractions and diversions to us, like butterflies to a soldier.

This usually does not mean becoming a hermit or turning your back on the things of this

world. It certainly does not mean ceasing to work
in and for the world. Brother Lawrence prac-
ticed this "renunciation" in the kitchen, amid his
worldly work, not in his monastic cell. This "renunciation" is not physical, it is not "changing
our works" but changing our hearts. It is also
called "detachment"—like "detaching" a fly from
flypaper. The fly is our soul, and the flypaper is
creatures. Both the fly and the flypaper are good
things, since God created them; but the fly is not
free to fly to God if it is stuck on the flypaper.
We are not free to love God insofar as we are
enslaved to creatures. And we all are. We are addicted to whatever we cannot part with that is less
than God, our true good. And that includes ourselves—especially ourselves and our own will. So
we must renounce this too, this especially.

God's world is not the problem; our attitude is.
God does not want us to renounce the unspeak-
ably beautiful world he gave us *as creation*, as gift,
as it really is. He wants us to renounce it *as creator*, as our god, as it really is not. This wonderful
world is our God-given house to live in and to live
the love of God in. But God's bride must learn not
to love her house as if it were her husband.

This "detachment" and "renunciation" of the
world are not an elite "higher way" for monks
and mystics; Christ clearly says it is a necessity
for all his disciples: "Whoever of you does not

renounce all that he has cannot be my disciple" (Lk 14:33). So we cannot avoid it. We have to understand it, and we have to do it.

Brother Lawrence explains the reason for it very directly: "Let us renounce, let us generously renounce, for the love of Him, all that is not Himself; *He deserves infinitely more*" (Letter 9). The hymn writer Isaac Watts put the point this way: "Were the whole realm of nature mine, that were a present far too small. Love so amazing, so divine demands my heart, my life, my all" ("When I Survey the Wondrous Cross").

Brother Lawrence recommends "one hearty renunciation of everything which we are sensible does not lead to God" (Conversation 4). This does not mean only one single once-for-all act; it does not exclude, but includes, many little repetitions of it throughout life, as being married includes many repetitions of the choice once definitively made, and as the Christian life means the continual renewing of our baptismal promises. But at least once in life we need to make a promise of "all", and not go back on that promise.

Brother Lawrence further describes his renunciation in these words: "What I sought after was nothing but how to become wholly God's. This made me resolve to give the all for the All, so after having given myself wholly to God, I renounced, for the love of Him, everything that was not He, and I began to live as if there was none but He and I in the world'' (Letter 1).

Brother Lawrence here is echoing Saint Augustine. In his *Soliloquies*, Augustine imagines the following dialogue between God and his soul:

God: What would you know?
Soul: Only two things.
God: What are they?
Soul: Yourself and myself. God and the soul, nothing more.
God: Nothing more?
Soul: Nothing more.

But Augustine was one of the busiest and most active saints in history. ''Only God and the soul'' does *not* mean ignoring the world or being insensitive to it. It means just the opposite of unrealism, ignoring the real world; it means realism, seeing the world as it really is. And what it really is, is a highway on which God comes to us and we go to God. Everything in this world is a Between, a relativity. It is relative to God and to us. Everything except God and us is such a Between, for it is between God and us. At one end of this Between, this highway, is the divine I AM, the Absolute. At the other end is his created image, the human self, which also utters the sacred word ''I AM''. Nothing else exists except the universe, which is only the large and complex road between these two, and fellow travelers, both humans and angels, on this road.

This is realism. We do not usually see reality so clearly, because our brains are scrambled by our addiction to creatures, as drug addicts are addicted to their drug. Brother Lawrence advises us to go "cold turkey" by "one hearty act of renunciation of all that we are sensible does not lead us to God". This is excellent advice, but I think God also offers other, more gradual "drug rehabilitation programs" for us cowards and fools who are unwilling to take the sudden treatment.

It is easy to understand why God calls us to renunciation. It is utterly reasonable. It is like giving up a cup of tea for the Hope Diamond. In the words of the Protestant martyr Jim Eliot, "He is no fool who gives up the goods he cannot long keep for the good he cannot ever lose" (*Through Gates of Splendor*). Or, in the words of the prototype of all martyrs, "What shall it profit a man if he shall gain the whole world and lose his own soul?" (Mk 8:36, KJV). No man ever uttered a more practical sentence than that.

15

SUFFERINGS

How to Transform Bitterness into Sweetness

Brother Lawrence assures us that "sufferings will be sweet to us while we are with Him, and the greatest pleasures will be, without Him, a cruel punishment to us" (Letter 7). What transforms sufferings and makes them endurable and even "sweet" is his presence. Therefore prayer, which is the practice of his presence, is the most practical and powerful answer to suffering.

God does not *cause* sufferings. In Job, it was Satan, not God, who took away Job's possessions, children, and health. All good is God's gift, and God does not destroy his own gifts. Suffering comes from sin, both actual sins and Original Sin. But God *uses* suffering for our good, our sanctification, and thus our eventual joy. Christ is our paradigm here, as everywhere: he never *imposed* suffering, and he *healed* many suffering people, but above all he *used* suffering, he embraced it, and transformed the meaning of it on the Cross.

The only reason we can accept sufferings is because they are not ours only but his, because in deliberately allowing us to suffer he puts us on his Cross *with him*. That is the key, that is the heavenly thing: "with him". For that is the very essence of Heaven: to be with him.

A man deeply in love with an extremely difficult woman was asked why he did not leave her, since she made him so unhappy. He replied, "Better unhappy with her than happy without her."

If you truly love someone, you do not love him as a means to the end of your own happiness. What you love is not your happiness, or your freedom from suffering, but *him*, and his presence, and oneness with him. Insofar as sufferings are part of that oneness, they are embraced too, and even loved— not for themselves, of course, but for the context they are in, like the villains in a great play or the dark shadows in a great painting, or the cacophonies in a great symphony.

Everyone who seriously pursues the love relationship with God eventually experiences some of the "sweetness" of the sufferings inherent in this way of life. For Christ has promised to all his disciples both parts of this "package deal", both the sufferings and the sweetness: "You will be sorrowful, but your sorrow will turn into joy" (Jn 16:20). "In the world you have tribulation; but be of good cheer, I have overcome the world" (Jn 16:33).

To speak of "the sweetness of sufferings" sounds strange, shocking, and perhaps even sick to those who do not know Christ, or know him only superficially. And even for his lovers, it usually takes some time to understand this. At first, suffering is far from sweet, even while we are "with him", that is, practicing his presence. Through much of our life with him he lets us taste the bitterness of sufferings without giving us many "sensible consolations" (as the saints call it) to overcome this bitterness, because he does not want us to get a spiritual "sweet tooth". He trains us to rely on faith instead of feelings. And here is where faith is most crucial: in suffering.

Everyone knows that suffering is a test of faith, but not everyone knows why. The reason is that while we are suffering, at first the suffering does *not* draw us closer to God but tempts us to turn away from him and to concentrate wholly on ourselves, in fear or self-pity. This is the worst thing about sickness: not the pain in the body but the narrowing of interests in the soul. It is as if the pain is a tyrant with a whip saying "Look at me! Look at me!" every moment.

That is why suffering is a test of *faith*, not just of courage to endure suffering. For a strong-willed person without faith can also have courage to endure suffering. But why do the faithful accept their sufferings from God's mysterious hand? Only because of their faith. These sufferings do not *feel* Godlike, and they do not *look* Godlike, and they do not make rational *sense* as Godlike. Only by faith do we know that God loves us, notices us, and even bleeds with us for love. Only by faith do we know that God has written our own name on this bloody love letter that is our suffering, has providentially designed this suffering for us (not *caused* it but deliberately permitted it) precisely *because* he loves us. That idea sounds utterly absurd, even reprehensible to people without faith. Yet we know it is true, and we know that only by faith. It is faith that sees it every time we look at a crucifix.

In fact, faith reveals the utterly logical character of what seems outrageously illogical to the faithless eye. If we only accept three premises about God's character by faith, then one of the most startling statements ever uttered follows as the logically necessary conclusion. If God is all-good, all-wise, and all-powerful, then "all things work together for good to them that love God, to them who are the called according to his purpose" (Rom 8:28, KJV)—even the most inexplicable sufferings. For if God is all-good, he wills only our good, never our harm; and if God is all-wise, he never errs about what our true good is; and if God is all-powerful, he accomplishes all that he wills. There can be neither indifference, nor ignorance, nor impotence in God. The only "escape clause" from all things working together for our good is our own free choice to reject and depart from his will. But if we do not, if we keep the lifelines of faith, hope, and love tied between God and ourselves, then it is absolutely necessary and absolutely logical that all things must work for good for us. Not everything that happens is good in itself, of course, but everything that happens "works for" our good. The worst thing that ever happened, deicide, the crucifixion of God, worked for the greatest good of all, our salvation. If he can work the greatest evil for the greatest good, he can certainly work lesser evils for lesser goods. If he could do it with his own Son's sufferings, he can do it with ours. He turns "Black Friday" into "Good Friday".

The sufferings he permits for us are like medical operations. The pain is necessary, though we do not understand why because we are not the doctor. What makes our faith in the Doctor more than a blind leap in the dark is the fact that he has suffered far more than we. He is the "Wounded Surgeon" (T. S. Eliot). Our faith in him is based, not on our desperate "will to believe" (William James), our own subjective wishes, but on the objective fact, the *deed*, of the Cross.

Suffering tempts us to deny one of the three premises, one of the three divine attributes of goodness, wisdom, or power. Usually it is God's goodness and love that we doubt, since we know, deep down, that we do not *deserve* the love of a Perfect Being, despite all our pop psychologists' patronizing, pandering, and positive pats. God would have been completely just, completely justified, if he had *not* gone to the infinite expense of sacrificing his own beloved Son to the pains of Hell itself on Calvary just for us. But he *did*: "God so loved the world that he gave his only Son" (Jn 3:16). *That* is what our faith is based on. That is why we believe God never neglects us, even when he seems to: because we believe in Christ.

That is why we believe that God never lets us fall into the fire, even when he seems to, but is really plunging us into the fire to forge our souls into beautifully Christlike swords. We believe this because we believe in Christ. That is why we believe God is using suffering to strengthen us even when it seems that it is weakening us: because we believe in Christ and his paradoxes about the weak being strong and the strong being weak.

God does not let the sufferings taste sweet to us from the beginning, because if they did, they would not test and strengthen our faith and thus increase our capacity for eternal joy in Heaven. But once we exercise this faith habitually; once our faith becomes like an anchor that stubbornly holds fast on the bottom of our soul even while storms disturb its surface, its feelings; once we say "God said it, I believe it, and that settles it", even when our bodies are in pain and our emotions in turmoil, God can then give us sweetness in suffering without weakening our faith. Believe me, he gives us sweetness as soon as he can, which is as soon as we are capable of it.

And this is the sweetness that comes from lovers' joy in sacrifice: "Can I really do that for you? Can I really give that up for you? How wonderful! All my love is for you, not for that, so giving up that is no sacrifice at all, but part of love itself, and therefore joy."

Dorothy Sayers writes,

The creative [God-like] will does not choose suffering, but It will not avoid it, and must expect it. We say that It is love, and "sacrifices" Itself for what It loves; and this is true, provided we understand what we mean by sacrifice. Sacrifice is what It looks like to other people; but to That-Which-Loves, I think it does not appear so. *When one really cares, the self is forgotten, and the sacrifice becomes only a part of the activity.* Ask yourself: If there is anything you supremely want to do, do you count as "self-sacrifice" the difficulties encountered or the possible activities cast aside? You do not. The time when you deliberately say, "I must sacrifice this, that, or the other" is when you do not supremely desire the end in view. At such times you are doing your duty, and that is admirable, but it is not love. But as soon as your duty becomes your love, the "self-sacrifice" is taken for granted, and whatever the world calls it, you call it so no longer.

Paradoxically, when we renounce our demand for sweetness and consolation, and in faith embrace our sufferings for God's sake, God gives us a far, far greater sweetness and consolation than we have ever experienced from the earthly delights we have renounced, *in* the very act of offering up our sufferings to him. Brother Lawrence observes, "Those who consider sickness as coming from the hand of God, as the effect of His mercy, and the means which He employs for their salvation [sanctification]—such commonly find in it great sweetness" (Letter 11).

If we insist on sweetness instead of suffering, we will find suffering in the very sweetness that we willfully demand; but if we renounce sweetness and accept sufferings for him, we will find sweetness in the very suffering that we faithfully accept. If we renounce the suffering we fear for the sweetness we seek, we will find the suffering we fear, not the sweetness we seek. Our very demand for pleasure will bring us pain, as any addiction does. Even Buddha knew that. It was his "Second Noble Truth": that the cause of pain is the desire for pleasure. The way of Christ is the only alternative. The Way of the Cross and renunciation is not one "extreme" that can be avoided without falling into the other "extreme", the selfish desires that lead to suffering. There are only two ways of life, in the end, and they are Heaven's way or Hell's way, "thy will be done" or "my will be done".

All the saints say, as Brother Lawrence does, that "God is often nearer to us, and more effectually present with us, in sickness than in health" (Letter 11). Why else would a loving God permit sickness instead of health? Lovers do all that they do for love—that is, for the good of the beloved and for increased intimacy. If we believe this, and if what we seek first is God's Kingdom in our hearts, that is, God's most effectual and most intimate presence, then all other things will be added to us (Lk 12:31); that is, we will be able to thank God for our sicknesses and sufferings. Faith sees behind the ugly scalpel the Surgeon's hand, and it is the hand of Infinite Beauty.

Brother Lawrence says, "Comfort yourself with Him who holds you fastened to the Cross. He will loose you when He thinks fit" (Letter 11). Notice that Brother Lawrence does not say, "Comfort yourself with the *thought* that . . ." but

"Comfort yourself with *Him*." No thought, not even the infallible proof of the truth of Romans 8:28 above, can comfort us when we are on a cross. Only his real presence on our cross can comfort us, for his presence on our cross means our presence on his.

The "Westminster Confession" begins with this uniquely Christian comfort:

"What is your only comfort in life and in death?"

"That I, both in body and soul, both in life and in death, am not my own but belong to my faithful Savior Jesus Christ."

Romans 8:28 — For we know that in all things, God works — ...

16

PATIENCE

Forgiving Ourselves for Failure

If you are serious enough about prayer and sanctity to be reading this book, I will wager that one of the most difficult virtues for you is patience —patience with yourself, with your repeated failures. Here is Brother Lawrence's advice to you. You will probably feel it is surprising, suspect it is impractical, and fear it is too easy, too good to be true. Yet I think it is a very practical and very holy attitude.

Brother Lawrence describes an impatient friend in these words: "She seems to me full of good will, but she would go faster than grace. One does not become holy all at once" (Letter 9).

This desire to "become holy all at once" is probably even more common in our modern world than in Brother Lawrence's medieval one, because we are used to technology giving us instant solutions, quick fixes, fast foods, and instant gratification. But sanctification is like baking a cake; even the great saints needed time to "cook".

Patience, like every virtue, is simply realism. In this case, it is the acceptance of the reality of *time*. Spiritual life, like physical life, grows gradually, like a plant. It cannot be made, or constructed, all at once, like a building.

We cannot "go faster than grace". We must be what Simone Weil calls "*waiting* for God". And we must *expect* his timing to be mysterious, for he is God. His mind is not our mind (Is 55:8). He is our Master, not our servant. If he did what we expected and when we expected it, like a good servant, he would not be God.

Brother Lawrence says, "He will come in His own time, when you least expect it" (Letter 3). His first coming into our world two thousand years ago was so incomprehensible and unexpected that *no* one understood him. All who ever met him were amazed: his enemies, his friends, and those who did not know whether they should be his enemies or his friends. His second coming, at the end of time, will be equally unexpected and equally amazing. And his continual comings to our soul between his two comings to our world, his continual graces, will not violate this pattern. He simply does not arrive "on time", as judged by our schedules, because he is a lover, not an airplane.

There are two parts to patience. First of all, patience concerns *time*. It does not demand instant gratification. Second, patience concerns _failures_. It expects and deals with failures. Brother Lawrence says, "When I fail in my duty, I readily acknowledge it, saying 'I am used to doing so; I shall never do otherwise if I am left to myself.' If I fail not, then I give God thanks, acknowledging that the strength comes from Him" (Conversation 2).

It is the first part of this confession that will probably strike you as questionable: not his attitude toward his successes but his attitude toward his failures. "When he failed in his duty, he confessed his fault, saying to God, 'I shall never do otherwise if You leave me to myself. It is You who must hinder my falling and mend what is amiss.' After this he gave himself no further uneasiness about it. . . . He was very sensible of his faults, but not discouraged by them" (Conversation 2).

You may think this sounds too easy, too cavalier, almost indifferent. But why? To be "sensible" of our faults but not "discouraged" by them is not indifference, it is patience. Not to be sensible of them, or not to confess them, is the road to pride. But to be discouraged by them is the road to despair. Brother Lawrence's attitude is not a compromise between pride and despair, for it is no less sensible of faults than despair is yet no less free of discouragement than pride is. How can we attain this state, of being sensible of our faults but not discouraged by them? By seeing our faults but also seeing farther than our faults; by framing our faults by our faith, which is not faith in ourselves but faith in God. No fault, no sin, no failure can exhaust God's power to forgive.

"See? That's what I will always do if you leave me to myself!" This strikes us as cavalier only because we are thinking about our sins the way the devil wants us to rather than the way God wants us to. God wants us to worry about our sins *before* we sin; the devil wants us to worry *after* we sin. God wants us to feel free after we repent (for we really *are* free then); the devil wants us to feel free before we sin, as we are choosing to sin (for we really are *not* free then; the devil is a deceiver). The devil tempts us to cavalier pride before we sin and worrisome despair afterward, since pride and despair both separate us from God, and *anything* that separates us from God is the devil's friend and our enemy, while anything that brings us closer to God is the devil's enemy and our friend. But what is our friend at one time can be our enemy at another.

What our Heavenly Father wants us to do about our spiritual failures is like what our earthly father wants us to do about our earthly failures. When we fall off the horse, or the bike, or the high road to Heaven, we must simply climb on again as soon as we are aware of the fact that we have fallen off, rather than sitting there stewing in self-

so true

pity or self-hatred. And remember to thank God for the awareness of the fact that you have fallen off the "horse" of awareness of his presence, for that, too, is his gift, not your achievement. If he did not give you the grace to notice that you have forgotten his grace, you would not only forget his grace, but you would also forget that you had forgotten his grace. And then your state would be without hope.

Test it out in your own experience: Does following Brother Lawrence's advice after you fail move you farther away from God or closer to him? And does self-hatred bring you closer or keep you away?

It does not really matter what our attitude is toward ourselves, whether it is positive or negative, except insofar as that helps or harms our relationship with God. There is only one thing necessary, and it is not a certain relationship to ourselves but a certain relationship to God. God is the unchanging absolute, not us. Sometimes we need to emphasize the negative in our relationship with ourselves and sometimes the positive. Self-confidence at the wrong time is pride, and self-deprecation at the wrong time is despair.

Timing is everything. A new preacher was to give his first sermon to his Scottish congregation. Full of self-confidence, he strode to the pulpit, head held high—and promptly forgot what he had planned to say. After a few fumbling minutes, he ended prematurely and walked out, head bowed and humbled. As he passed a wise old parishioner, she commented, "If ye had cum in the way ye went oot, ye cud ha' gone oot the way ye cum in."

"I shall never do otherwise if You leave me to myself" is simply realism and humility. Brother Lawrence does not say it in the spirit of blaming God for not giving him the grace. He knows the saying of Brother Giles in *The Little Flowers* of Saint Francis: "Who, think you, is the readier: God to give grace or we to receive it?"

Brother Lawrence shows in this saying that he has understood what Saint Paul understood when he said that "I know that in me, that is, in my flesh, dwelleth no good thing" (Rom 7:18, KJV). All evil comes from us, all good comes from God. If all evil does not come from us, some of it must come from God, and then God is not God but half God and half devil. If all good does not come from God, then God is not God but only *a* god, like Zeus, one of many sources of good.

This insight into our utter fallenness and helplessness is not despair. Precisely because all good comes from God, good comes from us, too, because God is so good that he shares his goodness with his creatures. God is charity, not selfishness. He builds us up when we least deserve it but most need it (as we should also do to each other). God is just the opposite of a miser who sees his children as rivals for his riches or a king with an ego problem who is jealous of his ministers; he loves to exalt his subordinates. Thus the Catholic emphasis, so scandalous to conservative Protestants on Mary and the saints, on a visible Church and material sacraments, on natural reason and natural law and the goodness of human nature and human free will.

The theological formula for this truth is that "grace perfects nature", including human nature, as a good father perfects his children. The gifts of nature that we receive from God, beginning with our very existence, are wholly dependent on his grace. But the same is true of our free choices: they are also his grace! In fact, the good we freely choose is even more a gift from God than the good we passively receive, since God's primary work in us is to perfect our nature, and our nature is freedom. Because grace perfects nature, the more our choices are God's, the more they are ours.

If you do not understand this wonderful paradox, it does not matter. God understands it, and that is what matters. He is the Playwright, not you. You are only the player.

17

GRACE

What Everything Is

Brother Lawrence says, "the greater perfection a soul aspires after, the more dependent it is on divine grace" (Conversation 4). You are aspiring to a greater perfection; that is why you are reading this book. Your heart is in love with a high ideal: God's perfect will for you. The only means great enough to attain such a great end is grace. It takes a divine means to attain a divine end.

The less we want grace, the more we need it. The more sinful we are, the more we rely on ourselves and the less we rely on God's grace—and the more desperately in need of it we are. The more saintly we are, or the more saintly we aspire to be, the less we rely on ourselves and the more we rely on God's grace. The devil relies on grace not at all; Mary relied on it totally.

"Everything is grace", said Saint Thérèse. This is neither pious exaggeration nor false humility; it is utter realism, the confession of clear and certain fact.

Realism means knowing reality and living accordingly. Realism means conforming our subjective reality to objective reality. The objective reality here is our total *dependence* on God's grace, in fact. The right subjective response here is our total *reliance* on God's grace, in faith. Faith is founded on fact. Faith is our response to fact. Faith is realism. The fact is that we *stand* on God as our only foundation. The faith is that we *rest* on God as our only foundation. We must rest on what we stand on.

Grace is the First Cause. Nothing causes grace. Nothing can cause God's acts of grace except God, the uncaused Cause. However, we can and must do something to receive this grace. We cannot cause or generate sunlight, either, only receive it; yet we can choose to go outside, where it is, or stay inside, where it is not. And there are ways, or methods, to go outside. Usually, the nearest door is best. There is no point in multiplying methods or using strange and elaborate ones like climbing up the chimney. The same is true for prayer and sanctity: there is a very simple method for going outside into the Sonlight, just as there is a simple method for going outside into the sunlight. Just as there is a door, there is a Man who said, "I am the door" (Jn 10:9).

Christ is the Mediator and channel of all grace. He is the complete and final Word of the Father.

Without him, all methods and human efforts are worthless. He told us that: "Apart from me you can do nothing" (Jn 15:5). Once we accept that, he becomes our method.

Prayer is not some interior technology, or self-manipulation, or spiritual button-pushing. It is simply standing in the light of objective reality. When we pray, instead of trying to produce love in our souls toward God, we should be basking in God's love for us. How foolish to stay indoors in the cold, dark little room of the self, trying to turn on the light and turn up the heat, when we can just go outside into God's glorious Sonlight and receive his rays! How silly to fuss with artificial tanning salons and lotions and lights when the Son is out!

Trusting God's grace means trusting God's love for us rather than our love for God. For "in this is love: not that we loved God but that he loved us" (1 Jn 4:10). Therefore our prayers should consist mainly of rousing our awareness of God's love for us rather than trying to rouse God's awareness of our love for him, like the priests of Baal on Mount Carmel (1 Kings 18:26-29).

Our prayers are often foolishly full of fussing efforts like Martha's and empty of quiet trust like Mary's. We try too much and trust too little. Count the times God's Book tells us to "try". Now count the times it tells us to "trust".

Brother Lawrence uses a remarkable image for our being carried by God's grace when he says, "Those who have the gale of the Holy Spirit go forward even in sleep" (Letter 4). The Spirit is a "gale", and we are sailboats. Faith is our sail. If we just put up the sail, we can catch the gale. Even when the sailors are asleep on their boat at night, the wind does not sleep but blows on the sails and moves the boat forward.

In some ways the Spirit can move us even more effectively in sleep than in waking, as surgery can be more effective when the patient is anesthetized. When we are awake, we keep hopping about on God's operating table, telling him how to doctor us. Only death quiets us enough for the radical heart surgery we need. Sleep is an image of that.

Since the Spirit blows also in our sea of sleep, we must prepare to catch this gale by evening prayers. Since sleep is like death, we should prepare for sleep as we prepare for death, by giving God eager permission to enter the sleeping sea-depths of our souls. In sleep, as in death, it becomes clear that "everything is grace."

Brother Lawrence describes the saint's attitude to God's grace in terms some will find shocking: "Hold yourself in prayer before God like a dumb or paralytic beggar at a rich man's gate" (Letter 5). This is simply realism, for that is what we are and what God is. We are like an old dog who has no higher happiness than to sit at his Master's feet. This is also called "humility". Saint Augustine, asked to name the four cardinal virtues, replied: "Humility, humility, humility, and humility."

High and holy ambition—to be a saint—is not opposed to holy humility—total reliance on God's grace. Exactly the opposite.

Ambition without humility is ambition that fails. It is pride, which goes before a fall (Prov 16:18). Humility without ambition is false humility. In fact, it too is pride, for it rebels against God's command to strive for "the upward call of God" (Phil 3:14).

We need grace to pray because prayer *is* grace. To pray is to be "wholly borne by God's grace", in the beautiful words of the *Catechism* (CCC 490) describing Mary. Prayer is spiritual surfing, soul-surfing on the waves of grace.

18

PERSEVERANCE

The Realistic Fanaticism

Patience and perseverance are two aspects of the same virtue, which is fidelity, or faithfulness. We sometimes mistakenly think of patience and perseverance as opposites because we think of patience as resignation and perseverance as stubbornness— as if patience were almost despair and perseverance were almost pride. In the same way, we mistakenly think of holy humility and holy ambition as opposites, when in fact they are two complementary aspects of the Godlike soul. God is both humble and ambitious, "easy to please but hard to satisfy". He is simultaneously patient and persevering, gentle and persistent, like water wearing away rock. The strongest forces in the universe, both physical and spiritual, always have that Godlike character. It is only because our minds are fallen and broken in two that we break this character in two and use two contrasting words for it.

Brother Lawrence says, "There is needed fidelity in those drynesses or insensibilities in prayer

by which God tries our love to him; *there* is the
time for us to make good and effectual acts of resignation, whereof one alone will oftentimes very
much promote our spiritual advancement" (Conversation 1).

Surfers can make progress paddling out to sea
only during the troughs between waves. We can
make progress in the daily and hourly paddle out
to God's depths only if we make efforts during
our spiritual troughs.

The reason is that only the will, or the heart,
can accept dryness and emptiness and suffering;
the feelings simply cannot do this. And despite
what unbelieving psychologists may say, our feelings are not the most precious and personal part
of us. They are the waves. We are the water. Feelings, like waves, look more substantial than they
are.

The only way God can strengthen his presence
in our will is to weaken his presence in our feelings. Otherwise we would become spiritual crip-
ples, unable to walk without emotional crutches.
This is why he gives us dryness, sufferings, and
failures.

While he can come to our feelings or to our
external sight without our will, he cannot come
into our will without our will! So the presence of
God Omnipotent to his beloved bridal chamber,
the human heart, must wait upon our free con-

sent. He will seduce our spirit, but he will not rape; he will not use force. He knocks upon the outside of the door of our heart, but the door opens only from the inside. If you look carefully sometime at that famous painting of Christ with the lantern knocking on the outside of a door, you will notice that there is no knob.

I think there are three exaggerated new fears that in our modern culture deter us from perseverance, and thus from holiness: the fear of violence, the fear of losing time, and the fear of fanaticism.

1. Brother Lawrence says, "Be not discouraged by the repugnance which you may find in it [prayer and sanctity] from nature; you must do yourself violence" (Letter 6). If we love our bodies, we must do violence to the diseases that are doing violence to them. If we love our families and our country, we must defend them against violent aggression by violence if necessary. If we love our souls, we must do violence to all the spiritual diseases or spiritual aggressors that are doing violence to our souls: laziness, lust, fear, self-pity, egocentrism, and whatever else in our fallen nature fears and turns from prayer.

Let's be utterly honest. Why don't we pray more? Why do we give up so easily? What is that voice that whispers in our ears, as soon as we begin to pray, "Why don't you wait just a little while?

You really need to do *this* or *that* first." There is
something in us that fears prayer as a maggot fears
light. We must do violence to this voice, for it is
not ourselves. It is our Enemy.

2. One of the suggestions of this voice of the
Enemy is that prayer is a waste of time. Brother
Lawrence recognizes this, and says, "At first one
often thinks it lost time. But you must go on, and
resolve to persevere in it to death" (Letter 6). For
our relationship to God is the whole meaning and
point of all our time. We *must* give the loaves and
fishes of our time (that is, our life, our life-time) to
him, for only he, the Creator and Master of time,
can save and multiply the time we give him, just
as he multiplied the little boy's loaves and fishes
(Jn 6), and as he multiplies his own Body in the
Eucharist.

If you wake up tomorrow morning and say,
"I have so little time today that I can't afford to
pray", you will not have time to accomplish the
things you sacrificed prayer for. But if instead you
say, "I have so little time today that I can't afford
not to pray", you will find at the end of the day
that somehow you accomplished more than you
could explain. God really performs the miracle of
multiplying our time—but only if we give it to
him first.

3. Finally, if there is anything Americans fear,
it is "fanaticism". Yet if there is *nothing* we can

be so "fanatical" about as to "resolve to persevere in it to death", we are already dead. And so are our promises, especially our marriages. Do we still mean "Till death do us part"? Do we even say it any more? And if we no longer make *that* promise, what promise can we be trusted with?

You become one great somebody only by one great love. What the world calls fanaticism, the saints call fidelity.

Winston Churchill gave the shortest and most memorable commencement address in history, at his alma mater during World War II. It consisted of just one sentence: "Never, never, never, never, never, never, never give up." Churchill's "never" was only for his battle against Hitler; ours is for our battle against Satan. His was only to save England; ours is to save our eternal souls. His ally was only the armies of America; our ally is the armies of Heaven (see 2 Kings 6:15–17).

How long must we persevere in this life of practicing God's presence and becoming holy? "To death." Nothing this side of death will make us stop. And when death does make us stop, we will then truly begin.